GREECE

FROM EXIT TO RECOVERY?

—

GREECE
FROM EXIT TO RECOVERY?

THEODORE PELAGIDIS
MICHAEL MITSOPOULOS

BROOKINGS INSTITUTION PRESS

Washington, D.C.

The Brookings Institution is a private nonprofit organization devoted to
research, education, and publication on important issues of domestic
and foreign policy. Its principal purpose is to bring the highest quality
independent research and analysis to bear on current and emerging policy
problems. Interpretations or conclusions in Brookings publications should
be understood to be solely those of the authors.

Library of Congress Cataloging-in-Publication data is available.
ISBN-978-0-8157-2577-0

9 8 7 6 5 4 3 2 1

Printed on acid-free paper

Typeset in Sabon

Composition by Cynthia Stock
Silver Spring, Maryland

For

MARK (T.P.)

and for

VERONICA (M.M.)

Contents

Foreword

Sipping a lemonade on a perfect summer evening, near the Acropolis in Athens in 2005, I was thinking about how beautiful and lucky a country Greece was. Greece's growth performance over the post–World War II period had been one of the best in the world, and per capita income had reached US$21,700 at market prices in 2005, making it a high-income country. More recently, the ratio of Greek to German per capita income had gone from 52 percent in 1995 to 64 percent by 2005. Greece had become a full member of the European Union and of the euro zone. The terrible period of right-wing military dictatorship and violence in the late 1960s and early 1970s was long gone, and democracy was functioning, in a somewhat populist and chaotic but perfectly peaceful way. There were no internal ethnic or regional conflicts, so prevalent elsewhere in the Mediterranean and Balkan regions. Thanks to the work of George Papandreou and Ismail Cem when they had been foreign ministers of Greece and Turkey, respectively, relations between the two neighbors had greatly improved, particularly since a special Greek rescue team was dispatched to Turkey by Greece immediately after a devastating earthquake in Turkey in 1999. It is amazing what such a gesture—and it saved Turkish lives—can do to promote peace and goodwill. Turkey reciprocated at the time of a smaller earthquake in Greece, some months later. Tensions in the neighborhood had decreased.

Greece was an influential member of the European Union and of NATO and, at the same time, had good relations with Russia, the Arab world, and Israel, as well as countries further afield. The adoption of the euro had gone well, growth had accelerated further, sovereign interest rates had fallen to almost German levels, and, at the time, IMF and European Commission economic reports were, on the whole, upbeat, as noted by the authors of this book.

Nobody foresaw the crisis that hit in 2008–09. Yes, there had been worries and warnings about the budget deficit, appearing to be in the 6 percent to 10 percent of GDP range in the precrisis years. The current account deficit was even higher, well above 10 percent of GDP already in 2006 and close to 15 percent of GDP by 2007. But many argued, as they did about Spain, that current account deficits in a monetary union are not relevant or meaningful magnitudes. After all, who worries about the current account deficit of Missouri or the surplus of Texas? Some today use a similar argument to claim that the German current account surplus of close to 7 percent of GDP is irrelevant. The budget deficit was considered more worrisome. But in 2008, Greece's stock of public debt was below Italy's as a percent of GDP. Even at the end of 2009, after the government acknowledged that some of the public finance statistics had been false, the ratio of public debt to GDP was not much higher that of Italy.

So why this devastating crisis? And, more important, how to rebuild strong momentum toward growth and prosperity for the future of Greece? These are the key questions asked by Theodore Pelagidis and Michael Mitsopoulos in this book. The research was a major part of our work on Europe in the Global Economy and Development program of the Brookings Institution and was generously supported by the Stavros Niarchos Foundation. Cooperation with ESADE in Spain and the Bosch Foundation in Germany allowed key pan-European workshops to take place.

In this foreword, I do not want to summarize the book, nor do I want to endorse or contest the various arguments or conclusions put forward with conviction and skill by the authors. Some of these arguments very usefully summarize existing analysis; others, however, are quite new. What is clear is that the Greek crisis was the result of multiple causes coming together with most destructive consequences. The world financial crisis triggered by Wall Street in 2008 meant that risk appetite collapsed on a global scale: economic indicators that seemed mildly concerning but manageable became much greater sources of alarm everywhere. The fierce political competition between New Democracy and PASOK that characterized the first decade of the new century had resulted in a degree of populism, particularly when it came to budget policies and employment in the public sector, policies that had pushed levels of indebtedness into the danger zone above 100 percent of GDP. Unlike Italy with its high domestic savings rate around 21 percent, Greece's savings rate was only around 14 percent of GDP, as reflected in the current account deficit. This huge current account deficit, far from being irrelevant, was an indicator of vulnerability to foreign capital flow reversals, as it always is. Competitiveness had been eroded, as was the case in other southern European countries by rapidly rising unit labor costs, on account of rapidly rising wages without matching increases in productivity. To top it all off, the Greek government had to admit that the fiscal accounts it had transmitted to Brussels and the IMF in the middle of the decade were not accurate. At that point, anxiety about Greece became contagious, and the current account deficit of Spain, previously considered irrelevant, became the great worry of most analysts. Then the Irish banking crisis hit, again surprising the markets, which had celebrated the amazing success of the Celtic tiger. What started as a Greek crisis turned into a crisis about the very functioning of the euro zone.

If Greece had been a non-euro zone emerging country like Brazil, Turkey, or Mexico, the International Monetary Fund program put in place would have included drastic austerity measures on the fiscal front. It would have been accompanied, however, by an immediate export-enhancing nominal devaluation of the national currency, which could have acted as a kind of short-term shock absorber by allowing an immediate increase in export demand to compensate for domestic cuts. Nominal exchange rate adjustment also acts as an automatic coordinating mechanism that decreases in real wages and production costs without the need for politically more painful and difficult to coordinate case-by-case nominal cuts.

Exiting an existing and functioning currency union is, of course, much more difficult than allowing an independent currency to devalue. I believe that the costs of an exit would have been even more devastating for Greece than the cost of the very imperfectly designed and implemented adjustment program. What made the situation in Greece much worse than it had to be, however, was the "talk" of exit, when exit really was not possible for economic but also more purely political reasons. For more than two years, this Damocles sword was left hanging over a country in deep suffering because the key actors, abroad and at home, would not or could not take decisive enough actions. The Greek people have had to pay a very high price for the uncertainty generated jointly by lack of domestic political compromise and a nationally agreed strategy, lack of decisiveness at the management level of the euro zone, and the lingering after-effects of the subprime mortgage crisis that fanned out over global financial markets from its epicenter in New York.

As this book is going to press in late spring 2014, Greece and Europe may have arrived at a turning point. In Greece, there are the beginnings of hope. The current account deficit in the balance of payments has vanished and a small primary surplus has appeared in the budget. Most important, there may be positive GDP growth in 2014 and 2015 for the first time since 2008. In the euro zone as a whole, there is also likely to be aggregate growth of about 1 percent in 2014, compared to a contraction of 0.5 percent in 2013 and a contraction of 0.7 percent in 2012. Few talk of euro exits any longer. Germany, appearing economically healthier than ever, finally is experiencing significant growth in wage and domestic demand, raising hope that its current account surplus may decline, which would help the overall internal rebalancing of the euro zone.

The social suffering in Greece and the crisis countries remains heartbreaking and politically unsustainable, however. I am not one of those who argue that such suffering was necessary to overcome the crisis. More decisive national policies and more courageous and timely euro zone actions could have avoided the depth of the recessions, in Greece and elsewhere in Europe. Theodore Pelagidis and Michael Mitsopoulos's book also takes this position. I agree wholeheartedly with them on this, but we cannot prove it, because one cannot perform counterfactual experiments with history.

It is all the more important, therefore, to look ahead. It is very useful to learn lessons from experience, but Greece should not waste energy on retributions for the past. The year 2014 indeed should become a turning point for both Greece and Europe as a whole. Pelagidis and Mitsopoulos show in the latter part of the book what avenues for growth there are in Greece, both in building on existing and remaining strengths in shipping and tourism, as well as in turning to new, high technology and skill-intensive sectors. Moreover, we live in an ever-more interconnected world. The more the euro zone will succeed as a whole, the more Greece will succeed. And the more Greece starts to grow again and is able to reduce its debt and unemployment burden, the more successful the euro zone will become as a whole. Countries such as Spain, Italy, and Portugal will benefit from Greece's success as it will send the message that the crisis in the European periphery is over, and investment funds will come. Neighboring Turkey will benefit from increased Greek demand as well as more prosperous Greek visitors. Germany will benefit from Greece's growth, as it will show that Europe as a whole and Germany, its leading economy, can deal with regional difficulties and that Europe is again full of promise as a path-breaking economic and political peace project. And, of course, Greece desperately needs the success of Europe and its neighborhood so that it can export, receive more tourists, and generate employment at home. Success, as well crisis, is geographically contagious.

The Global Economy and Development program at the Brookings Institution is glad to have been able to help organize this work on Greece and Europe with the financial support of the Stavros Niarchos Foundation. We are grateful to the authors. I believe they have made a very valuable contribution to the analysis of the Greek economy and its challenges and to the discussion about the future.

I do hope that in the summer of 2015, a year from now, I will again sip a lemonade in Athens or on one of the beautiful Greek islands, happy to see that the worst part of the crisis is indeed over and to sense optimism in the summer breeze. There is no guarantee of a strong recovery yet. A lot remains to be done, by Greece, of course, but also by Greece's friends and Europe as a whole.

KEMAL DERVİŞ
Vice President and Director, Global Economy and Development
The Brookings Institution

Acknowledgments

We would like to gratefully acknowledge the Stavros Niarchos Foundation for its support. We wish to thank Kemal Derviş, Jacques Mistral, Javier Solana, Josep Borrell, Domenico Lombardi, Guillermo Vuletin, John Page, and Karl-Heinz Paqué for comments and discussions on earlier drafts of the manuscript, as well as Stelios Vasilakis of the Stavros Niarchos Foundation for his comments and ideas throughout the project. We also thank the participants of the Brookings workshop in Washington, D.C., on September 13, 2012; the Brookings-ESADE workshop in Madrid on March 12–14, 2013; and the Brookings-Bosch workshop and conference in Berlin on May 23–25, 2013, for providing comments and ideas that advanced the quality of the book. Last but not least, Brookings has provided an excellent environment for work, exchange of ideas, and academic reflection.

Brookings recognizes that the value it provides is in its absolute commitment to quality, independence, and impact. Activities supported by its donors reflect this commitment, and the analysis and recommendations here are not determined or influenced by any donation. Interpretations or conclusions in all Brookings publications should be understood to be solely those of the authors.

List of Abbreviations

AMECO	Annual Macroeconomic Database of the European Commission (http://ec.europa.eu/economy_finance/db_indicators/ameco/index_en.htm)
BERD	business expenditure on research and development
BoG	Bank of Greece
B-P test	Breusch-Pagan test of heteroscedasticity
CDF	cumulative distribution function
EA	euro area
EC	European Commission
ECB	European Central Bank
EFSF	European Financial Stability Facility
EIB	European Investment Bank
ELA	emergency liquidity assistance
EMI	European Monetary Institute
EMU	European Monetary Union
ESA	European System of National and Regional Accounts (followed by the European Commission for its official records and statistics, or Eurostat).
EU	European Union
Eurosystem	European Central Bank and the national central banks together constitute the Eurosystem, the central banking system of the euro area

FDI	foreign direct investment
FGLS	feasible generalized least squares (estimation)
GCR	Global Competitiveness Report
GDP	gross domestic product
GERD	gross expenditure on R&D
HFSF	Hellenic Financial Stability Fund
ICT	information and communication technology
IKA	Idrima Kinonikon Asfaliseon (Greek social security fund for private sector employees)
IMF	International Monetary Fund
INSEAD	Institut Européen d'Administration des Affaires (European Institute of Business Administration)
IPO	initial public offering
MFI	main financial institution
MP	member of parliament
NACE	Nomenclature statistique des activités économiques dans la Communauté européenne (European statistical classification of economic activities)
OECD	Organization for Economic Cooperation and Development
OLS	ordinary least squares (estimation)
OMED	Organization of Mediation and Arbitration
PSI	private sector involvement
R^2	coefficient of determination
R&D	research and development
SMEs	small and medium enterprises
SURE	seemingly unrelated regression equations
VAT	value added tax
VIF	vector inflation factor
UN	United Nations
WEF	World Economic Forum
WGI	World Governance Indicators

GREECE

FROM EXIT TO RECOVERY?

Introduction

This book attempts to identify strategic mistakes in the adjust-ment program of Greece and in that way to identify the improvements needed to achieve the ultimate and desirable goals of both improving the living standards of the Greek population and ensuring the solvency of the Greek sovereign. To do so we draw both on historical precedent and on an analysis of the more recent developments. Then we attempt to provide some additional insight into growth-enhancing policies that have yet to be explored in efforts to identify growth potential for the country. The first chapter explores the process that led to the accession of Greece to the euro area, a decision that many, both inside and outside of Greece, now question. Nonetheless, it is useful to recall what Greek politicians thought as they put the country on the path to accession, despite the numerous weaknesses and challenges already obvious at the time. Similarly, it is helpful to review the weaknesses that accumulated after accession and led to the current crisis, as well as document how the IMF and entities within the European Union tracked and responded to these developments. The insights resulting from this process can deepen our understanding of the current situation and suggest policy choices that have the potential to turn the economy around. One major insight in particular emerges: the problems now facing Greece and Europe appear to arise less from the conditions of the Greek economy at the time of its accession to the euro area and more from an inability to deal with the problems that existed beforehand and new challenges that emerged after the accession, in the context of the monetary union.

Chapter 2 analyzes the various sectors of the economy, in particular the specific characteristics of labor costs within each sector. The official lenders to the Greek government emphasized, sternly and consistently, the need for a significant "internal devaluation," meaning a reduction of incomes and asset prices in general, rather than an increase in the nonlabor cost-competitiveness of the country. This was a controversial strategy from the outset, and it continues to be so. Today, the old Greek paradox of "rapid growth in spite of the low national competitiveness" has been replaced with the new Greek paradox of "faltering exports despite falling wages." The strategy of driving down wages to increase competitiveness was focused aggressively on "internally devaluing" the private sector; however, the pressure to apply this constraint to the public sector was much weaker, especially during the critical 2010–12 period. Even worse, an effort to substantially reform the public sector, in particular, during the same period was not a priority. Understanding why this strategy failed to secure the desired outcomes is still important since it can help correct a fundamental flaw in the design of the Greek adjustment program while there is still time to do so. An understanding of both the developments in the Greek financial sector and the qualitative aspects of the internal devaluation is critical for an understanding of how the costs and risks caused by the inability of the Greek government to implement a useful reform agenda were pushed onto the Greek private sector. This approach, which sought to reduce private sector wages, employment, and profits while gradually allowing the emergence of a full-blown liquidity crisis— in a country with a very hostile business environment, extremely high administrative burden, and much increased energy prices—had, in the end, rather limited beneficial effects.

In the third chapter, we focus on how the support of research-based innovation can restore competitiveness to the Greek economy, without relying on the suppression of labor costs. The aim here is not to provide a comprehensive growth strategy for Greece.[1] Rather, we select a topic that has not been studied by such efforts so far and concentrate on research and development activities by businesses. We are motivated by research from Hausmann and others (2011), McKinsey (2012b), and the World Economic Forum (2013), among others, that argues that an efficient and diverse manufacturing base connected with research centers is essential for the development of a modern, competitive economy. It needs to be stressed that support for research-driven manufacturing does not need to come at the expense of support for sectors that are usually identified as growth drivers for Greece, such as tourism and shipping—even when the economy is competing for scarce resources and capacity. On the contrary, there are numerous opportunities to enhance both, for example, by reviving manufacturing activities related to the shipbuilding industry or creating opportunities for medical tourism.

In particular, we investigate why Greek companies spend so little on research and development (R&D)—an issue that has received little attention from researchers who are suggesting ways for the Greek economy to grow. We examine the role of R&D for two principal reasons. First, existing studies and literature strongly indicate that research-based innovations play an increasingly crucial role in the ability of an economy to maintain a competitive manufacturing base, which in turn appears to be a prerequisite for maintaining a competitive economy that can support a high standard of living. Second, Greek policymakers often point to the low R&D expenditure of Greek companies while calling for them to increase it. However, if the R&D expenditure of Greek companies is constrained by the policy environment in which they operate rather than by corporate strategies and choices, then policymakers must remove these bottlenecks if they want to improve the competitive performance of the country in this aspect; this holds especially since there is compelling evidence that these bottlenecks hamper a mutually beneficial collaboration between the noteworthy state-financed research capacity available in the country and the business community.

A review of the extensive literature reveals numerous conditions that must be met to create an environment conducive to innovation—in particular to research-based innovation. This review is complemented with our observations on the current reality in Greece, based on the collection and evaluation of hard data, examination of related laws, and numerous interviews with innovative entrepreneurs and researchers over the past five years. The analysis of available data further corroborates the assertion that policy variables crucially affect R&D performance in the private sector. We conclude with a number of specific policy proposals for those key areas where policy initiatives could help reverse the current unfavorable situation and restore the competitive edge of the Greek economy by fully exploiting the potential of existing assets.

From La Dolce Vita *to Collapse*
The Sins of the 1990s and 2000s
That Led Greece into Free Fall

The emergence of the current crisis and the way it has been handled by successive Greek governments once markets lost confidence in the Greek sovereigns has caused many opinion leaders and academics to doubt the wisdom of the Greek participation in the European Monetary Union (EMU). Similar doubts have been expressed about the decision of the European Union to accept Greece into the EMU.

This chapter addresses three aspects of these questions and doubts. The first one deals with whether the Greek politicians who put Greece on the path to accession were aware of the challenges the country would face and whether they thought that they had a strategy to address these challenges and make Greece's participation in the EMU worthwhile both for the country and for the European Union (EU) as a whole.

The second question is directly related to the possibility of addressing these challenges today. A thorough analysis of the legacy of the 1990–93 period—when the decision to join the euro area was made—documents the emergence of the factors that brought Greece more than a decade of fast growth. It also demonstrates the failure to end the nexus of special interest groups that thrive on the very practices responsible for the low competitiveness of the country and that even today are able to effectively undermine the reform agenda. These anticompetitive practices affect price and employment levels and corporate profits, among other things. An examination of the earlier pattern of fast growth—despite of the anticompetitive environment fostered by these special interest groups—enables us to identify the numerous paradoxes that undercut the applicability of widely cited statistics in the case of Greece.

A final question investigated in this chapter is what the international organizations, now the official lenders of Greece, believed both before Greece's accession to the EMU and thereafter. This applies especially to the perceived weaknesses of the country and the chances that these could be addressed before the onset of grave consequences, such as the current crisis.

Ratification of the Maastricht Treaty by the Greek Parliament

Here we offer a historical analysis of the views Greek politicians expressed with respect to the anticipated costs and benefits that would follow Greece's accession to the EMU, and the prospects of realistically minimizing the risks and costs of the structural and fiscal imbalances within the country. Since assessment of such costs and benefits is usually based on the theory of optimum currency areas, we also offer a summary of that theory.

The views of Greek politicians about the ability of the country to deal with its structural and fiscal imbalances and to adjust to the demands of a single currency area are drawn from the positions they expressed publicly in the Greek parliament during sessions that preceded the voting of key laws and the approval of the annual budget as well as important sessions such as the one preceding the vote of confidence for the incoming government in the early summer of 1990 and the ratification of the Maastricht Treaty, all of which are meticulously documented in the archives of the Greek parliament. This material was further supplemented by author interviews with key politicians from that period, a detailed reading of the relevant laws enacted back then, and the use of confidential material; although the last cannot be quoted, it was used to verify otherwise publicly available information.[1]

It should be noted here that the government that introduced the Maastricht Treaty to the Greek parliament for ratification in 1992, but lost its majority in the parliament in late 1993, remains very controversial in Greek public opinion and among prominent Greek opinion leaders and is rarely mentioned or referred to. As a result, this administration has rarely been studied (another effort to collect the available evidence that documents the economic thinking that shaped the understanding of the Greek policymakers and politicians who put Greece on the path to EMU accession is Featherstone, Kazamias, and Papadimitriou 2000). The evidence reveals what Greek politicians regarded as the costs and benefits for Greece if it were to join the single currency and explains their statements that shaped public opinion about European integration.[2] Today it is widely believed that the decision of Greece to join the euro area was made during 1998–99, when Greece fulfilled the inflation and deficit criteria set out in the Maastricht Treaty and consequently was invited to participate in the final stage of the EMU. The importance of satisfying these criteria should not be discounted. However, it was the summer of 1992 when the political system had to deliberate about whether it would be beneficial for Greece to join the effort toward deeper European integration and the establishment of a monetary union. This was the time when the critical decision regarding Greece's accession to the euro area was made.

Thus we start the analysis with the liberal government that lasted from summer 1990 until September 1993, not only because this government introduced the Maastricht Treaty for ratification to the Greek parliament during July 1992 but also because of its wide-ranging and ambitious strategy to implement structural reforms and rationalize public finances. This strategy was directly related to the government's narrative with respect to Greece's need to prepare itself adequately before the final stage of the EMU. Furthermore, the policy initiatives of this particular government bore a strong similarity to the structural reforms Greece was asked to implement as part of the conditionality program agreed upon in early 2010.

Two points must be kept in mind when evaluating the following material. First, the public speeches and actions of politicians are obviously driven by their political agendas and therefore often are not always well grounded in economic theory. Second, most members the 1990–93 parliament were doctors, lawyers, engineers, and officers of civil servant unions. Therefore, with few notable exceptions, they lacked the necessary background to argue effectively on economic cost-benefit terms with respect to the accession of Greece to the euro area, given that their staff also lacked the relevant knowledge based on financial and economic matters. Still, the interventions of those relatively few members of parliament (MPs) with the background to understand and argue constructively on the matter at hand, as well as the interventions of other MPs, provide information that allows us to explore their views with respect to the structural and fiscal challenges the country was facing.

Ratification of the Maastricht Treaty by Greece and the Economic Policy Context

The available material, which includes the discussion in the Greek parliament preceding the ratification of the Maastricht Treaty, reveals, on the part of Prime Minister Constantine Mitsotakis and the ministers directly involved in the shaping of fiscal and economic policy, an understanding of the significant structural and fiscal challenges the country would face in order to participate on equal terms in the common currency area.[3] In the end, the prime minister and leading ministers appeared to be preoccupied mainly with how the country would manage to truthfully meet the economic policy benchmarks, the "nominal convergence criteria" as they were designated at the time, set by the treaty to ensure a sufficient level of coordination of economic and fiscal policies in the common currency area. Furthermore, they believed that these challenges could be dealt with if the Greek government resolutely implemented an ambitious reform strategy, in particular one that removed the privileges handed out to interest groups through "regulatory favoritism." They argued that such privileges constituted a significant drag on economic productivity and had to be eliminated to ensure the future prosperity of the country, regardless of the EMU accession. It is also clear that this administration realized that failure to implement this strategy would have grave consequences for the country in any case, but especially within the single currency area.

According to the available evidence, the government appears to have firmly believed that it did have a strategy that could address the existing structural and fiscal challenges and that this strategy would be implemented during its term in office and beyond that. This view seems to be supported by an analysis of the laws introduced by the government during the 1990–93 period, which confirms that Greece was rapidly reforming even as it implemented a fiscal consolidation of unprecedented size. Net borrowing (excluding interest) declined from 5.1 percent of gross domestic product (GDP) in 1990 to 0.7 percent of GDP in 1993, as shown by the European Commission (EC 2013a) data presented in figure 1-1.

The structural reforms and legislative initiatives are also reflected in the evolution of the indicators constructed by the OECD with regard to product markets. The OECD indicators on product market regulation, and in particular for telecommunications, show how most other European countries moved ahead with deregulation primarily after the mid-1990s, something also revealed by a reading of the relevant laws introduced at the time in most European countries. When Greece moved ahead with the deregulation of the mobile telecommunications sector during the early 1990s and attempted to genuinely privatize fixed-line telecommunications, only the United Kingdom, among the major European countries, had already created a competitive telecommunications market. The deregulation of certain product markets during this period contributed

Figure 1-1. *Finances of General Government, Government Debt and Net Borrowing (without interest), Greece, 1970–2013*

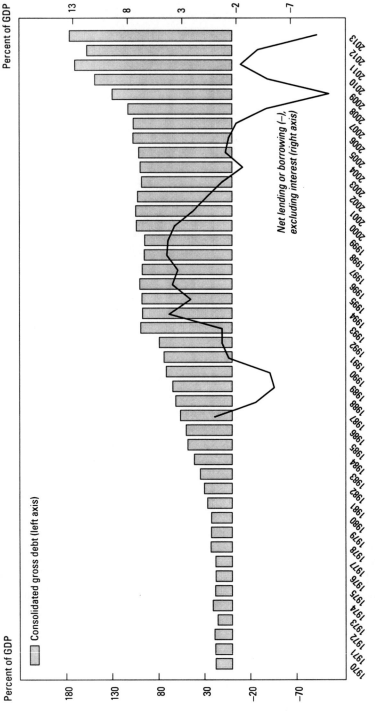

Source: EC (2013a, Part 2: tables by series).

significantly to Greece's growth performance after the mid-1990s, even though the level of regulation after 1993 was still very stringent compared to that in other OECD countries (Conway and Nicoletti 2006). It should also be noted that the documented improvement in this index—that is, less stringent regulation—mainly reflected the issuance of mobile communications licenses in the early 1990s.

As for the other key network industries mentioned in the government's policy statements at the time, the law establishing an electricity market was passed in Greece in 1993 to complement a competitive tender to establish the first private electricity producer in Greece. The case of the electricity production market in Greece is not as well known as the deregulation of the telecommunications market (which is notorious due to its connection with the fall of the government). But the fact that Greece was already attempting to introduce a competitive market for the production of electricity in 1993 is notable given that similar reforms were not effectively started in Germany and the Netherlands until 1998; in Sweden, Finland, Italy, Belgium, and Spain such electrical sector reforms were not initiated until 1996, 1995, 2004, 2007, and 1995, respectively. Only the United Kingdom had started that process earlier, in 1990.

Among the regulatory reforms attempted or implemented in 1990–93, many were ultimately halted or reversed by subsequent governments. The privatization of the Athens bus lines, the deregulation of private hospitals and diagnostic centers, and the revision of the legal framework for strikes are indicative examples. But some reforms endured, such as important changes in company law; competitive tenders for marinas and casinos; the abolition of numerous price controls (including on fuel and bread, rents, and real estate agent fees); liberalization of bakeries, domestic air routes, and the fertilizer market; and creation of competitive markets for private insurance and chartered accountants.

In other cases, even before the fall of the Mitsotakis government in October 1993, progress was not commensurate with the ambitious goals set by the government. Thus numerous smaller obstacles to doing business—along with some flagship reforms like those affecting road haulage—were not addressed during the short term of the government, possibly deferred in anticipation of a second term that never materialized. And in spite of some key successes, a strategy to improve human resource management in the public sector had little visible impact. Even within the government, there was open resistance to this effort to reinstate accountability and to improve other aspects of human resource management;

and the political opposition at the time actively encouraged resistance to reform from within the public administration. With the fall of the government, this reform effort ended prematurely; therefore implementation of this key initiative cannot be properly assessed. It remains, however, a prime example of how the government's strategy did not always secure the desired results during its term. It also demonstrates the power that rent-seeking interest groups had obtained from the mismanagement of the country, and how they succeeded in staring down a small but daring group of politicians determined to protect the interests of the public and rein in the profits of the interest groups.

To judge the credibility of the 1990–93 government's assertions that it had a plan to address the significant challenges faced by the country, one also has to assess the implementation of its fiscal consolidation strategy. The general government data tables, published by the European Commission (figure 1-1), show a fall of about 5 percent of GDP in the deficit of the general government budget excluding interest to GDP.[4] This figure as well as those from other sources cited in this section demonstrate both the daunting challenges and successes of the implemented policies. Despite unavoidable failures, overall these policies managed to stabilize a situation that was clearly leading the country to the reality it eventually faced after 2010. The size of the problem faced by the government at the time is demonstrated by the fact that the Greek government actually had additional debts and liabilities, amounting to 30 percent of GDP, that simply had not been recorded as part of the official debt.[5] As a result of acknowledging these debts, the ratio of government debt to GDP increased from 79 percent in 1992 to 99 percent in 1993 (see figure 1-1). The magnitude of the reform efforts undertaken is most clearly shown by the size of the fiscal consolidation and the fact that the final expenditure on salaries of public sector employees actually decreased as a percentage of GDP during the Mitsotakis government. The government objective to reduce the ratio of public debt to GDP to within the permissible limits of the debt criteria of the Maastricht Treaty was explicitly acknowledged to be extremely ambitious but considered feasible if the government made a determined and persistent effort to achieve it.

With regard to the opposition, it took an understandably negative stance, largely motivated by political tactics. But beyond that, key members of the opposition pointed out the crucial macroeconomic weaknesses in the design of the single currency area as well as the associated risks that could arise, both for weaker member states and for the union as a whole—especially if a member state failed to satisfy a sufficient level of economic policy coordination within the euro area. And that issue was quite separate from the need for Greece to implement progressive structural reforms to positively adjust to the realities of the common currency area. Whatever the motives of the opposition politicians, they did point out the dangers to the union stemming from the inability, within a common currency area, to address regional shocks with fiscal constraints for each member state in the absence of an effective central fiscal authority. The opposition pointed out that there was an inherent asymmetry in the system, which had a centralized monetary policy, deficit, and debt limits but no matching central fiscal authority. Once a country joined the monetary union, it would have no ability to execute countercyclical policies to address regional shocks—providing of course that its before-crisis debt and deficit levels were not excessive.

Members of the opposition also criticized the structure of the monetary union in the context of Europe's north-south divide. They argued that without such a fiscal authority in Brussels, Greece would stagnate, unemployment would increase dramatically, and labor income would remain low. Furthermore, they asserted that handing the European Central Bank (ECB) the sole mandate to combat inflation by exercising a centralized contractionary monetary policy would add to unemployment and poverty in the EU periphery, potentially amplifying the differences between rich and poor regions and making the path to the EMU a dead end for all southern countries. Germany's postunification transfers to its eastern half were often cited by opposition MPs as they argued for a federal structure of the EU that had to be completed quickly, so that the union's responsibility for using fiscal tools to compensate for inequalities matched its power to make other policies within the single currency area.

In addition, they argued that as a result of the Maastricht Treaty fiscal ceiling, interest rates, exchange rates, and fiscal control in the common currency area would no longer allow fiscal stabilizers to function countercyclically and that, as a result, a national government would no longer be able to deal with a regional shock. They noted that in contrast the U.S. federal budget was large enough to act in such cases, but the budget of the European Community was so small that it could not play such a role. Some members of the opposition argued that this would pose a risk to weak countries, like Greece, and they suggested the creation of a central fiscal authority in Brussels that could perform that counterbalancing function in the weaker peripheral regions. As a result of these deliberations, most of the leading figures in the parliament agreed that the European Community budget had to be increased and that the "Delors Package" had to be fully paid up, as only then would a euro area membership be beneficial for Greece.[6]

Such views were based on the economic theory of optimum currency areas, which emphasizes the possibility of nonsynchronized, asymmetrical business cycles among member states. This is a theoretical consequence of the customs union process that tends to deepen market integration, which in turn reinforces differences in the structure of production and demand (Mundell 1961; Krugman 1993; Baldwin 2006). Thus the greater the differences in the structure of production, the greater will be the asymmetric incidence and magnitude of demand shocks on individual countries and regions.

In particular, when demand shocks are asymmetric, business cycles between two countries (for example, Greece and Germany) will be desynchronized. Desynchronization of business cycles means that Greece would experience, for example, a negative growth rate with relatively low inflation while Germany would experience, at the same time, a positive growth rate with low unemployment. In such a case, the two countries need diversified stabilization policies—both fiscal and monetary. Greece would require accommodation through low interest rates to stimulate economic activity, whereas Germany would need some contraction to combat potential excessive inflation—although Germany might require some reflation to help the deficit-bearing country stabilize.

This was exactly the situation many Greek MPs feared: asymmetric business cycles within the monetary union would not allow Greece to exercise a countercyclical fiscal or monetary policy. And that is why they were uncomfortable with the absence of any kind of fiscal union and a strong budget to permit Brussels to step in and fight a possible negative demand shock in the relatively poor European south.

Another concern among Greek MPs was that the ECB would tend to serve the strongest and core member states and thus might not intervene to accommodate peripheral member states hit by a negative shock. The opposition MPs in particular stressed the fact that in a situation like that, recession might be addressed by austerity measures, which would have a further negative impact on employment and GDP. On the other hand, most of the government representatives appeared confident that, with the right dedication and effort, Greece would be able to implement the structural and fiscal reforms needed to secure its position as a constructive equal in the monetary union, in spite of the flaws in the design of the European common currency area. There seemed to be a consensus in the Greek government that institutions had to be modernized and productivity had to be increased by the elimination of distortions, outdated practices, and unacceptable legal privileges for profit—all of which had prevented the economy from operating efficiently within the single market and the future monetary union. Prime Minister Mitsotakis and Finance Minister Stefanos Manos believed in the so-called credibility paradigm (Persson and Tabellini 1996): if Greece implemented the necessary reforms, it might overcome the disadvantages described by the theory of optimum currency areas and benefit from the unprecedented macroeconomic stability that adherence to the rules of the monetary union and the per se participation in it would secure.

It is also worth mentioning that those members of the opposition who argued most vehemently against the structural reform and privatization agenda of the government were subsequently found by Greek courts and the tax authorities to have accumulated wealth well beyond their official incomes, abused their offices, and accepted large bribes—mainly from foreign companies, according to the evidence thus far available (see appendix A).

Macro- and Microeconomic, Structural, Political, and Institutional Factors Leading to the Crisis, 1990–2008

The government that introduced the Maastricht Treaty to the Greek parliament fell before it could implement its vision to place Greece within the common currency area. This played a crucial role in the events that led ultimately to the current crisis.

The legacy of that government has two aspects. The first is positive, comprising a set of factors that supported the strong growth and macroeconomic stability that the Greek economy experienced from 1995 to 2008; these had their roots in the strategies implemented during the 1990–93 period. The second aspect is negative: the inability to eliminate factors that contributed the country's low competitiveness, institutional weakness, and poor governance. These factors remained unaddressed during the 1990–93 period because the government's efforts were undermined by special interest groups, the opposition in the parliament, and even elements within the government. The initial successes led ultimately to a spurt of fast growth. But the failure to confront the nexus of powerful rent-seeking special interest groups also meant that, despite this fast growth, the country was unable to deal with the deeper causes of its institutional failings—such as low competitiveness and poor governance—that had been festering and accumulating for decades.[7] The persistence of these factors ultimately led to the current crisis.

In this section we examine these two legacies and then analyze why production is more costly in Greece compared to the remaining euro area countries. This exploration confirms that Greece is one of those countries that was able to secure rapid growth for some time as a result of particular reforms and circumstances but failed to build the social and economic institutional capacity needed to maintain such growth over the long term (see Rodrik 2007, 2012). We argue that overcoming the resistance to reform from the country's various special interest groups remains a daunting challenge unto this day.

Structural Reforms and Macroeconomic Stability: The Causes of the Fast Growth from 1995 to 2008

In the 1950s Greece was the poorest country among its EU-15 peers in terms of per capita GDP, but by the mid-2000s the country had attained the average level of wealth among the EU-27 countries. This period can be broken down into three main phases. From the 1950s until the late 1970s, when the oil shocks tested the economy of Greece along with that of the rest of the world, Greece was the fastest-growing economy in Europe and one of the fastest-growing OECD member states (Maddison 1995; figure 1-2). This was a central argument for accepting Greece into the European Community, once political stability and democracy had been reinstated after 1974.

Then the long period of robust growth abruptly ended, and from 1981 until 1990, the country's growth rates were visibly lower—often negative. At the beginning of the 1980s, two main events occurred, distinct from the impact of the oil shocks. The first was Greece's accession to the European Community, the result of decade-long aspirations. But it also was an event that forced the Greek industries, accustomed to operating in a heavily regulated and protected environment, to face much stiffer international competition. Second, a new government was elected, one that adopted an aggressive policy of public spending increases (mainly in the public sector and in numerous social benefit programs). Although there were intermediate periods of fiscal contraction, such as in 1983 and 1985–87, public spending expanded unsustainably, and for the first time, the stock

Figure 1-2. *Real GDP Growth Rate, Euro Area and Greece, 1961–2013*

Percent, year over year

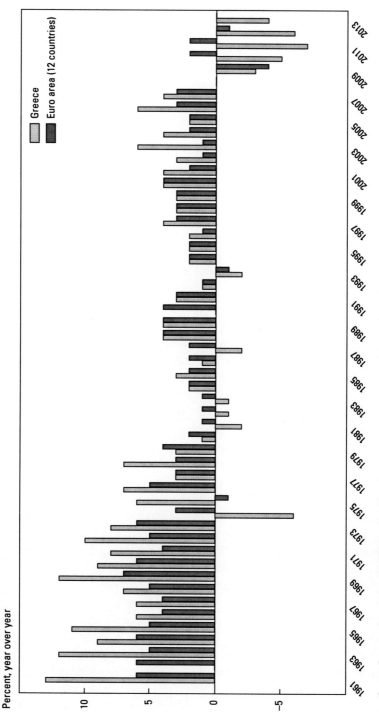

Source: European Commission, "AMECO Database" (http://ec.europa.eu/economy_finance/db_indicators/ameco/index_en.htm).

of public debt built up to dangerous levels, as reflected in the debt-to-GDP ratio presented in figure 1-1. The government further increased the role of the state in the economy, at a time when other countries gradually were doing the opposite. In addition, this government deliberately decreased accountability in public office as a means of ensuring its ability to replace preceding structures of political favoritism with those of its own. The entire decade of the 1980s was characterized by performance that was far worse than that of the other European countries as Greece adapted to lower levels of productivity, a shrinking or stagnant production base, and the consequent lower employment level in the private sector.

Finally, as a result of the 1990–93 efforts to stabilize public finances and reduce the stifling and inappropriate influence of the government and the effects of clientelistic politics on the economy, a period of strong growth began in 1995. It led first to a restoration of confidence in the economy and then to the macroeconomic stability ensured by EMU accession. This period of fast growth that followed the partial reform efforts of 1990–93 is very pertinent to Greece's current crisis, as during this time it seemed to many inside and outside the country that living standards in Greece would be able converge with those in the advanced European countries. However, it also was erroneously believed by many—as we now see with the benefit of hindsight—that Greece would be able to do so without reforming the special privileges that burdened the productive economy or without confronting the special interest groups that the 1990–93 government had openly but unsuccessfully confronted.

These observations are pertinent to the government elected in 2004, which won a large majority in parliament on an agenda of state modernization and rationalization of public finances. This government included many members of the conservative faction that had previously opposed the reforms of the 1990–93 period. Their continued unwillingness to undertake meaningful structural and institutional reforms ultimately led to a lack of a reforming zeal and, finally, to the failure to stabilize public finances that ultimately triggered the crisis. From 2004 to 2009, the large increases in government expenditure, public sector employment, and the public sector wage bill were particularly notable for exacerbating Greece's debt load, repeating once more the persistent patterns of the past. The 1990–93 period remained, therefore, the only exception in precrisis modern Greek history when government expenditures declined.

During the early 1990s, the drive to implement reforms and rein in government spending coincided with another global slowdown. But the performance of the Greek economy then, in spite of the large fiscal retraction, was not significantly worse than that of the other European countries. It was the determined drive, in this period, to push ahead flagship reforms and privatizations that helped restore the trust of the markets and European peers in the country, leading to the inflow of direct investment and the restoration of market access for the Greek government. Despite the sizeable fiscal adjustment, these key reforms kept the decline in GDP within bounds and formed a solid foundation for the nation's strong growth performance from 1996 up to 2008.

The strength of the forces that supported growth in Greece for such a long period is explained by the fact that Greece was at the time one of the few, if not only, economies to have ever experienced simultaneous financial sector liberalization and stabilization of the macroeconomic environment. This happened as the full liberalization of the credit markets (which began in the early 1990s and essentially finished by the decade's end) coincided with EMU accession. The ensuing expansion of private credit replaced fiscal deficits as the main way to finance the growth of consumption in Greece and allowed the private sector debt to increase even while the stock of the public sector debt remained at levels that posed visible risks to the country.

These demand injections, analyzed in Mitsopoulos and Pelagidis (2011), had an important impact for every year during a prolonged period that spans the duration of Greece's strong economic performance. Stabilization of the perceived macroeconomic outlook of Greece in the wake of EMU accession contributed significantly to the expansion of private credit, the interest rates offered by commercial banks to households and businesses declined, and concurrently the inflation differential between Greece and the euro area average fell significantly. The expansion of credit to households fueled the growth of private consumption during the years of fast growth (Mitsopoulos and Pelagidis 2011). In fact, the only time when credit-driven private consumption did not form the principal driver of growth was during the period preceding the completion of the infrastructure projects for the 2004 Olympic Games—an exception easily explained by the peak in the investment growth rate during that time.

In addition to effects of structural reforms and macroeconomic stabilization, large infrastructure projects, shipping, and the tourism industry also continued to contribute to the growth of the economy during this period. The last two industries constantly secured significant annual revenue inflows of up to 15 percent of GDP that were added to the domestic demand and helped mitigate the large trade balance deficit.

The fiscal stimulus of the 2004 Olympic Games effectively led to the speedy completion of key infrastructure facilities, mainly in the Athens metropolitan area. The rapid increase in new investment, both public and private, demonstrates the impact of the infrastructure investment, largely cofinanced by EU structural funds; these were started mainly during the 1990–93 period but had been amassed up to 2004—a clearly visible manifestation of growth. More important, many of these projects, like the Athens ring road and Metro, actively boosted the productivity of the economy in the greater Athens area, where about half of the Greek population lives. A survey by the Workers' Center of Athens (1997) documented the hours lost daily by employees during their commute, with the long duration of the commute being identified as a major problem (which matches the findings of numerous happiness studies). Thirty percent of respondents used public transportation, 30.5 percent drove their private vehicles, and 11.6 percent rode a motorcycle. For 25 percent of the respondents, their commute exceeded one hour, and the average commute was half an hour. A subsequent survey by the Ministry of Transport (2006) documented that 17.5 percent of the commuters using private means of transport in 2004 had switched to using public transport by the time of the survey. The same survey found that over 50 percent of working commuters used public transport at least two to three times a week; another 30 percent stated that they used it for their commute every day. Half of the latter used the metro. Over 500,000 trips were registered every workday by the operator of the Athens Metro, in a city of about 4 million residents. Similarly, data published by Attiki Odos (2010), the operator of the ring road, document a high perceived benefit from using it, with more than half the commuters saving between sixteen and thirty minutes per trip and more than 85 percent of the users gaining more than sixteen minutes. Usage peaked during commute times and at the time of the Attiki Odos survey averaged about 200,000 accesses to the ring road per day.

Low Efficiency and Competitiveness, Institutional Weaknesses, and Poor Governance

Other than the flagship reforms of the early 1990s, the institutions of the economy remained largely unchanged during the period of rapid growth. In fact, many of the reforms that had been implemented were later reversed to some degree, usually as a result of pressures from special interest groups. Following the fall of the Mitsotakis government in 1993, all subsequent governments up to 2010 proved very reluctant to directly confront the special interest groups. Successive governments swiftly removed the few ministers who tried either to rationalize the social security system or to pass reforms that would deregulate the economy and introduce elements of accountability into public administration. Thus the numerous distortions of the economy and the weaknesses of the institutions persisted and grew, as did the power of the many special interest groups that benefited from these distortions. They were able to secure and sustain a comfortable living based on rents that were financed by cheap credit and large inflows from the EU in the form of structural funds and Common Agricultural Policy payments for government-administered activities (Mitsopoulos and Pelagidis 2011).

Low Efficiency. Efficiency studies have documented the serious weaknesses that persisted in Greece preceding the current crisis. Country efficiency is a measure that compares the actual gross domestic output of a country with its potential, where the potential gross domestic output is estimated based on the best practices of its peers using the same type of inputs in their productive processes.[8] Greece consistently ranked very low among the OECD or EU countries, with an efficiency level of around 65–70 percent at an aggregate national level during the 1980s and 1990s (Arestis, Chortareas, and Desli 2006; Moomaw and Adkins 2000; Henderson and Zelenyuk 2007).

The sector-specific efficiency within Greece shows trends similar to those on the national level. Even the better-performing sectors such as education (Afonso and Aubyn 2005) or the public sector (Afonso, Schuknecht, and Tanzi 2005) still demonstrated lackluster efficiency, at 70–75 and approximately 78 percent, respectively. Such low efficiency in one of the largest sectors of the economy, such as public administration, or in one of the core sectors relevant to future growth, such as education, has serious long-term ramifications for the entire country, which is already suffering from endogenous and persistent shortcomings across its economy. Even though this may lead to a reading that the private sector is less inefficient than the public sector, the high inefficiency of sectors under strong public control, such as transportation, education, and electricity, undermines the efficiency of the private sector. Using the recent data from Eurostat, the analysis by Desli and Chatzigiannis (2011) estimated the efficiency of EU-27 countries versus Greece for the 1995–2008 period and found that the average efficiency for Greece was 71 percent versus 87 percent for the

Table 1-1. *Efficiency Level for Selected EU-15 Member States, 1995–2008*
Percent

Countries	1995	1996	1997	1998	1999	2000	2001	2002	2003	2004	2005	2006	2007	2008
EU-15	91	93	95	95	95	95	95	93	91	91	91	91	91	85
Germany	100	100	100	100	100	100	100	100	100	100	100	100	100	100
Spain	81	86	89	88	86	82	80	78	73	71	68	67	68	60
Finland	72	75	79	84	84	83	81	79	79	84	82	83	84	72
Greece	65	68	70	69	69	69	72	71	73	75	74	76	76	67
Ireland	100	100	100	100	96	91	88	79	79	77	77	75	78	71
Italy	100	100	100	100	100	100	100	92	88	85	84	83	85	73
Portugal	50	52	54	54	55	53	53	50	51	51	53	54	56	48

Source: Desli and Pelagidis (2012), elaboration based on efficiency data from Desli and Chatzigiannis (2011).

entire EU. Greece's low level of efficiency becomes even more apparent when it is compared to the average efficiency level of 92 percent achieved by the oldest EU-15 members that are peers for Greece.

In the late 1990s, Greece's annual efficiency level hovered around 70 percent (Desli and Pelagidis 2012, Desli and Chatzigiannis 2011). In the 2000s the efficiency level of Greece continued to increase while the average efficiency levels of the EU-15 and EU-27 were declining. This improvement was probably due to the same factors discussed previously, such as the deregulation of the financial and telecommunications sectors. The sharp reduction of the efficiency level of the Greek economy at the beginning of the financial crisis in 2008—by 9 percent for Greece versus only 6 percent for EU-15 members—demonstrates the underlying weakness of the preceding growth in efficiency. The detailed presentation of the efficiency levels of selected EU member states in table 1-1 illustrates how countries with ongoing financial troubles experienced a severe deterioration of their efficiency levels after the emergence of the financial crisis while certain countries, such as Germany, handled the financial crisis in a firm and resolute manner—at least during the first year. Portugal's efficiency seems to have fared worse than that of Greece during the entire 1995–2008 period, Spain's efficiency level deteriorated from 89 percent in 1997 to 60 percent in 2008, and the efficiency levels for Italy and Ireland followed a similar trend, falling to slightly above 70 percent in 2008. Overall, the average efficiency of the EU-15 area prior to the EMU accession was slightly higher, but after accession the average stabilized at 91 percent. Based on the efficiency studies, there might be other countries

Figure 1-3. *Inflation Differential between Greece and Euro Area 13, 1999–2007*[a]

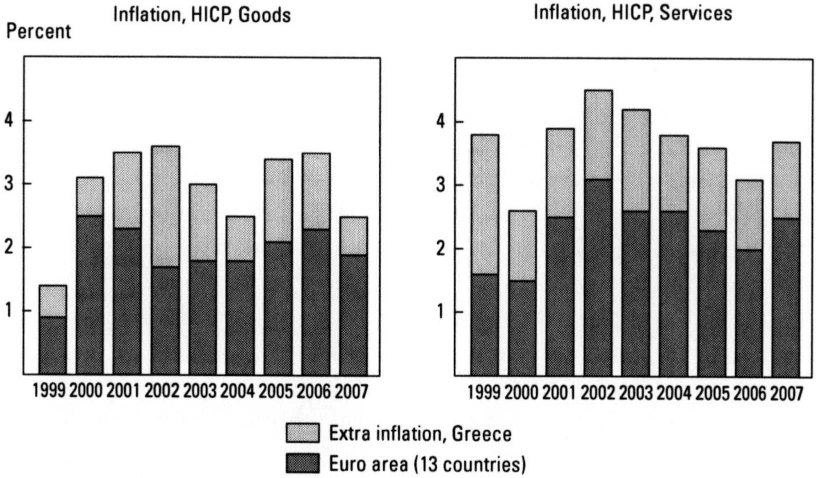

Inflation, HICP, Goods   Inflation, HICP, Services

Percent

Extra inflation, Greece

Euro area (13 countries)

Source: Authors' calculations using Eurostat database (http://epp.eurostat.ec.europa.eu/portal/page/portal/statistics/search_database), various years.
a. HICP, harmonized index of consumer prices.

among the EU-15 with efficiency levels consistently lower than the EU-15 average. The economies of those countries—such as Finland— may merit closer examination.

Low Competitiveness and Employment. After 2000 Greece had gained unprecedented macroeconomic stability and access to finance, and yet endemic rent-seeking by special interests had badly undermined the country's competitiveness. This poor competitiveness was manifested in four ways. The first was the persistent double-digit current account deficit as a percentage of GDP; at such levels this deficit invariably generated grave consequences for the country. The second manifestation of poor competitiveness was Greece's inflation rate, which was persistently higher than euro area average. Third, there was, and still is, the demonstrable unattractiveness of Greece as a destination for foreign direct investment, as reflected by the low level of net inflows that was, and still is, practically zero. Fourth, there emerged a wide range of characteristics that distorted the functioning of the labor market.

The inflation differential between Greece and the euro area (see figure 1-3) was a repeated concern among the IMF directors during the Article IV reviews of Greece. The interesting part about this differential was not its mere existence, which many had sought to explain as an example of the Balassa-Samuelson effect because of the rapid Greek growth rate—an explanation seized upon by Greek policymakers to distract from the root causes of the Greek inefficiencies. However, that explanation did not fit well: in particular, the inflation differential emerged both in the goods (tradable sector) and services (nontradable sector) subindexes, with a pattern that did not fit the Balassa-Samuelson argument, which states that the differential should be much stronger in the nontradable sector.

In addition, the trade and current account deficit in Greece clearly demonstrated a serious discrepancy between the growth of domestic demand and the increase of the domestic supply of both goods and services. Ultimately, the evidence makes it more appropriate to label Greece as a unique case of "quasi Balassa-Samuelson," where exports are replaced by European transfers and domestic credit expansion through external public and private borrowing, and the price level is pushed upward in both the goods and services sectors. This matches available research conclusions (Gibson and Malley 2007; Pelagidis and Toay 2007). The increase of the goods deficit follows as a natural consequence in this case, as increased demand is satisfied by competitive imported goods since there is no sufficient domestic supply of goods that can compete with the imports, especially within the single market for goods. In the case of Greece, participation in the euro area seems to have averted developments such as high inflation and currency devaluations that would have occurred sooner if such a trade imbalance and inflation differential had emerged in a country with its own currency.

The third manifestation of Greece's poor competitiveness was the country's unattractiveness as a place to do business, despite its fast growth. Data from the Bank of Greece indicate that the FDI rarely contributed to financial inflows, an observation in line with the link between the attractiveness of the business environment and FDI (see Hajkova and others 2007). Finally, since the strong demand growth was not being satisfied by an increase in domestic supply, employment remained unusually low (figure 1-4) despite years of rapid economic growth. This had a profound impact on Greek society. The newer generations entering the job market found very few—and largely unattractive—job opportunities. This in turn significantly distorted the productivity indexes that measure GDP to labor input. Since the increase in GDP was driven by strong demand and increased capital intensity, but with a limited increase in accompanying employment, these indicators showed a large increase in productivity per worker, or

Figure 1-4. *Employment Ratio for Those More than Fifteen Years Old, 1983–2012*

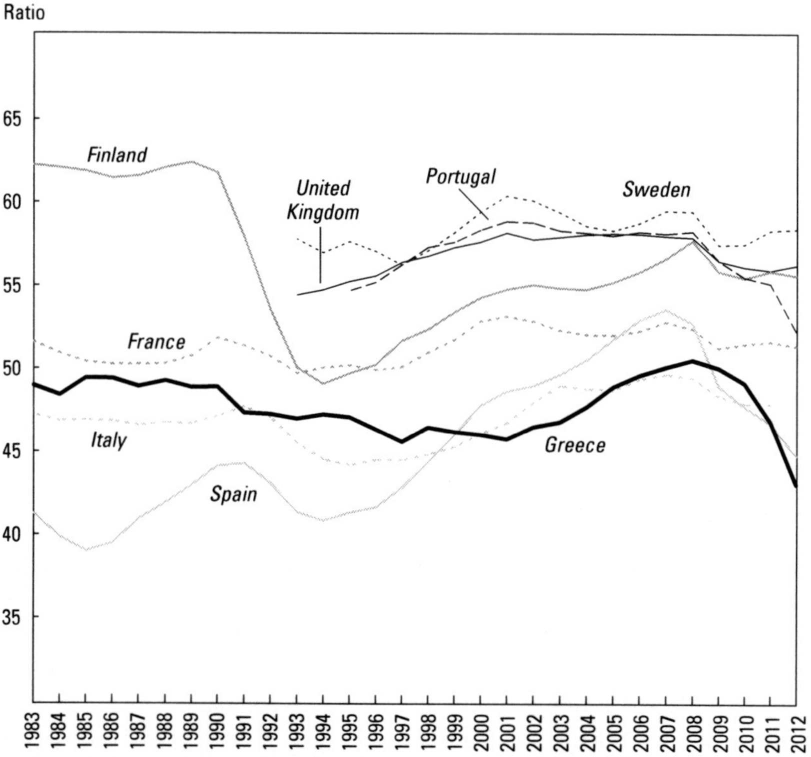

Ratio

Source: Authors' calculations from AMECO database (NETN)/(NPAN+NPON) (http://ec.europa.eu/economy_finance/db_indicators/ameco/index_en.htm).

per hour worked, in spite of the poor competitiveness and relatively low employment levels of the economy (Mitsopoulos and Pelagidis 2011).

This imbalance resulted in relatively high wage increases for the smaller number of employees in the Greek economy compared with other countries as well as increases in unit labor costs, even while the total wages in the private sector remained low as a percentage of GDP. The peculiarities of the labor market that emerged in this distorted environment are described in Mitsopoulos and Pelagidis (2011, 2012) and in the end may have contributed to the fact that even the official lenders of the country after 2010 never managed to obtain an accurate picture of reality and, consequently, of the measures needed to constructively address the causative distortions.

Institutional Weaknesses and Poor Governance. Greece's weak institutional capacity, relative to the level of its per capita income, has been widely documented by numerous surveys and reports, which include the World Bank Governance Indicators and Doing Business rankings, the OECD Indicators of Product Market Regulation Database, competitiveness surveys such as the Global Competitiveness Index compiled by the World Economic Forum, and surveys such as the Corruption Perception Index compiled by Transparency International.[9] It is noteworthy that a wide selection of different surveys, including those measuring governance and corruption, rank Greece roughly in similar ways, even though the methodologies used often differ significantly. This is consistent with the findings of Kaufmann and Kraay (2006). They suggest that an evaluation, such as the one undertaken here, should be based on both objective and subjective measures, and they document that the margins of error from using methods based either on hard evidence or the subjective responses to questionnaires are rather similar.

Thus it is not surprising that the aforementioned surveys and reports as well as the estimates of the EC (2006b), among others, all found that at the onset of the crisis in Greece, administrative costs were exceptionally high, regulation of markets was excessive, the regulation of professional services was high for entry and the pricing of services, and government intervention was limiting competition and hampering efficient resource allocation and pricing decisions in crucial network industries. At the same time, qualitative standards in professional services were found to be excessively lax (Paterson, Fink, and Ogus 2003), and the overall business environment was perceived to be unattractive.

The OECD Product Market Regulation Database indicators reveal the regulatory and institutional rigidities in the Greek economy.[10] They show the pattern of state intervention and high administrative costs that secure economic rents for those beneficiaries favored by Greek lawmakers. However, tracking the reforms implemented after 2010 poses some methodological challenges, since implementation often did not immediately follow the adoption of key laws that are assessed by these indicators. Duval and Elmeskov (2005) also stress the need to assess the implementation of reforms, even beyond the adoption of EU legislation at the national level.

These findings are supplemented by more general statements indicating weak institutions in addition to the unattractive business environment and poor governance (see Kaufman, Kraay, and Mastruzzi 2005; Kaufman and Kraay 2006). Figure 1-5 demonstrates how the high levels

Figure 1-5. *Corruption and Regulation, All Countries, 2006–07*

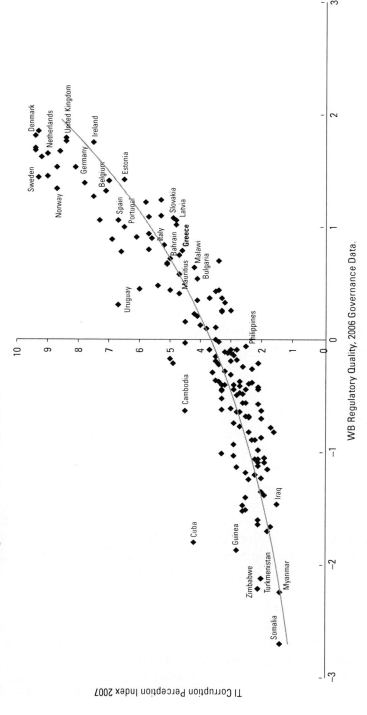

TI Corruption Perception Index 2007

WB Regulatory Quality, 2006 Governance Data.

Sources: World Bank, "Worldwide Governance Indicators" (http://info.worldbank.org/governance/wgi/index.aspx#home); Transparency International, "Corruption Perception Index" (www.transparency.org/research/cpi/overview).

of corruption seem to follow high administrative burden, poor governance, and overregulated product markets, as argued by the related literature (see summary by Lambsdorff 2006).

While combating tax evasion has been emphasized in the governmental rhetoric and policy priorities put forth by the official lenders to Greece after 2010, the problems of corruption and abuse of office seem to have received significantly less attention, despite the fact that they are crucial in ensuring the survival of interests groups that obstruct reform and thrive on dirty money. Similarly, until the onset of the crisis, prosecutorial emphasis was skewed toward simple tax evasion, which was actually punished more severely than abuse of office and the commitment of high crimes and misdemeanors.

Profits, Wages, and Potential Benefits of Reforms

All of this evidence illustrates why production is more costly in Greece when compared to the euro area, despite the fact that, as shown by reliable data from Eurostat and the EC AMECO database, even before the crisis, gross wage levels in Greece were more than 30 percent lower than the euro area average (see chapter 2) and by now are more than 40 percent lower, especially in those parts of the private sector that do not benefit from state-sponsored regulation that curtails competition.[11] Also, in Mitsopoulos and Pelagidis (2011), data from comprehensive databases of corporate balance sheets demonstrate how the high administrative cost measured in Greece (see chapter 2, figure 2-14) and the low profitability of Greek companies are congruent with the foregoing facts. This is how—as a result of high administrative costs and the costs of legal ambiguity and institutional insufficiency—consumer prices increase even as profits—measured with respect to turnover and assets—remain low. The reading of this evidence differs from widely used data from Eurostat and the EC that add the income of the self-employed to the value added by companies. Use of these data without qualifying that self-employed income is unusually high in Greece too often conveys a very misleading picture of supposedly excessive profits in the country. This error is compounded by the analysis of wage costs based on percentage changes and not on absolute levels, which leads many economists and policymakers to draw conclusions that are even more detached from reality. These grave errors in the reading of available statistics, which are analyzed in Mitsopoulos and Pelagidis (2011), have led almost all Greek policymakers and official lenders to assume, incorrectly, that "excessive profits" in Greece are one of the main reasons why prices are in some cases higher than in other European countries. An accurate reading of the situation would show that even in the numerous cases where competition is limited by legislation or state practices, higher prices do not lead, on average, to excessive profits but rather simply cover the cost of the inefficiencies caused by other legislation and the overall institutional weakness of the country.

It is therefore not surprising that Greece is the country with the most to gain in terms of increased productivity from fixing these problems, as suggested by Conway and Nicoletti (2006), Nicoletti and Scarpetta (2005), and the related subsequent work of the OECD Economics Department. Other studies using different methodological approaches have reached similar conclusions (see, for example, Mylonas and Papaconstantinou 2001; McKinsey 2012a). In fact, these endemic causes of economic inefficiency are a major factor in Greece's weak performance in other arenas, from research and innovation (Bassanini, Scarpetta, and Visco 2000) to environmental protection and the quality of public health services, schools, and institutions of higher education (see Bassanini and Scarpetta 2001; Sutherland and Price 2007). Even the poor and deteriorating performance of the judiciary, as documented by Djankov and others (2002) and Mitsopoulos and Pelagidis (2007, 2010a) can be ultimately linked to this environment of generally weak institutions.

Why Are Reforms So Difficult to Implement in Greece?

Earlier in this chapter, we argued that during the 1990–93 period, leading MPs across the entire political spectrum clearly understood the problems of the country. These key figures in the government appeared determined to implement the reforms needed for the economy to be ready to enter the euro area with a solid structural and fiscal background. This entailed widespread modernization of all institutions, including those of public administration. As the costs of the status quo were often stressed during the relevant parliamentary discussions, one might wonder what prevented these reform-minded politicians from implementing the changes necessary to render the country ready both to enjoy the fruits of joining the euro area and to minimize the costs, as described by the theory of optimum currency areas with which they were familiar. To answer that question, one must examine the important role of the powerful rent-seeking interest groups.

It is critical to understand the nature and extent of the alliances formed by these special interest groups to defend the status quo in Greece during the whole period under examination (see Mitsopoulos and Pelagidis 2009, 2011, 2012). As of this writing, six years since start of the crisis, these groups still act like "Vikings," grabbing anything they can while roaming freely through various areas of social and economic activity. At the same time, they defend their pockets of manipulative gain created by government regulation aimed specifically to create such rents by restricting free and transparent competition and by reducing transparency and accountability in the management of public funds. These rents benefit the many small but well-placed and well-organized groups that draw a significant advantage from their small size. These groups apply most of their available time and substantial influence defending their privileges of a comfortable income; they rationally invest time and money to influence policymakers and the administration. They form alliances of smaller groups that occasionally merge unofficially and on a case-by-case basis whenever their interests align to manipulate the system for additional gain or to defend their privileges. These groups take full advantage of the lack of checks and transparency in the system that would permit the public to object to such predation. The almost absolute overlap and solidarity of interests between the executive and legislative branch in Greece, as documented in Mitsopoulos and Pelagidis (2011), is only one attribute that removes checks and balances from the system. The fact that not all court decisions are published for public scrutiny nor are the minutes of parliamentary committees illustrates indicatively how the lack of transparency has been effectively and meticulously established in Greece.

In this environment manipulation for gain used to assume any convenient form. It was legal as long as legislation, passed effectively unchallenged, endorsed a benefit or restricted competition in a market so as to grant the special interest group privileged access to that market. But rent-seeking could also assume the illegal form of corruption. Thanks to the meticulous undermining of the rule of law, the interest groups considered illegal gains to be roughly as attractive as legal manipulative gains, "economic rents" in the classic sense. In these cases of illegal activity, the gains were obtained by blackmailing lawmakers and the executive and by explicit "horse trading" with the administration, based on the realistic assumption that no one would ever report such crimes, and in the rare event that someone did, there would be no punishment or effective sanction.

IMF and EU Assessments of Greece during the Accession Period (1990s) and the Golden Years of 2000–09

What do the IMF, EU, and ECB surveillance reports reveal about Greece—and these institutions' insights and oversights—from 1990 to 2010, a period that began with efforts to address the legacy of structural and fiscal imbalances from the 1980s and concluded on the verge of a major crisis? In these reports all the aforementioned fiscal and structural weaknesses had been identified along with the persistent inability of Greek governments to deal with cost control rather than revenue increases, at least at a general level. Yet these reports, especially from the IMF, often demonstrate a lack of detailed knowledge about various issues, for instance, the real problems of the Greek labor market.[12] In addition, while all these entities cautioned the government about the potential gravity of the country's imbalances, the timing of the strongest IMF warning in 1994 (IMF 1994) was very unfortunate, since it preceded the exact beginning of the period of strong growth.

The reports by the IMF suggest that it failed to appreciate the significance of linking structural reforms to fiscal consolidation efforts during the 1990–93 period, when Greece had last lost market confidence and was close to bankruptcy. It also apparently failed to properly assess the critical importance of a strategy combining structural reforms with fiscal consolidation efforts and protecting the property of private investors as a means of restoring confidence.

The process of Greek accession to the EMU, following the ratification of the Maastricht Treaty in 1992, was closely followed by the European Community, first, and then EU bodies and other international entities. Their documents indicate that the challenges the country was facing were well known, but by 2000 they were deemed to be manageable within the common currency area. The available material strongly suggests that it would have been impossible at the time to predict the extent of the subsequent policy failures and the catastrophic consequences they would generate.

The IMF, EU bodies, and ECB reports essentially state, albeit diplomatically, that consequent to the efforts of the 1990–93 period and the successful management of the EMU accession during the 1996–99 period, successive governments took advantage of the "windfall" of cheap interest rates and rapid growth that the previous structural reforms and EMU accession had secured while they consistently avoided tackling the remaining structural and fiscal challenges. At the same time, one legacy of the fall of the government in 1993 was a very strong signal to the political elite that there were immense costs to their personal careers if they insisted on meaningful reforms.

IMF Country Reports for Greece, 1990 until 2009

A comparison of the IMF Article IV chairman's summary for Greece for the 1990–93 and 2005–09 periods and the supporting staff reports reveals a very interesting fact: either the evaluation of the 1991–93 period seems relatively harsh or the 2005–09 evaluations seem relatively mild.[13] The first basically predicted immediate doom, and the second worried about the medium term until 2009, when "immediate action" was again explicitly called for. Clearly missing from the report for the earlier period is an assessment of the impact of the weak (at the time) conjecture of the international economy on the Greek economy, as well as the fact that in the midst of an unprecedented fiscal contraction, the Greek economy had actually performed no worse than it did in the previous years of fiscal profligacy—and no worse than the other European countries. While the IMF appears not to have taken note of this, at least at the level of the directors' summary for the Article IV missions, the government at the time was aware of this fact, which it attributed to the aggressive program implementation that had restored the trust of the markets in the country, as well as to the equal emphasis given to genuine fiscal consolidation and growth-enhancing structural reforms. Ultimately, the pursuit of these two goals may have had important implications. The predicted doom did not occur during 1994, and after 1995 the country performed strongly, facts that subsequently may have made the IMF reluctant to pursue a more accurate assessment of the dangers Greece was facing. And the IMF's failure to fully appreciate that structural reforms counterbalanced the effect of the fiscal contraction during the 1990–93 period appears to have recurred after 2010.

The detailed staff reports of the period are in line with the directors' conclusions. It is noteworthy that the ability of the Greek government to meet its targets is repeatedly questioned explicitly and forcefully during the 1990–93 period. In 1991 the IMF staff even complained that the government did not have a well-defined program. This contrasts with the actual cohesion between the government's inaugural policy statements, its key policy speeches in the parliament from early on in its administration, and its record of reforms implemented during its term.[14] Tellingly, the IMF staff questioned the government's ambitious infrastructure projects because of the scarcity of needed funds—an issue the government addressed via innovative contracting terms. The IMF staff also repeatedly questioned the government's medium-term macroeconomic targets, especially the fiscal consolidation effort and macroeconomic aggregates, such as inflation and growth after 1993–96. The government seemed firmly convinced that its policy of liberalization and privatization ultimately would lead to a steep decline in inflation and a strong rebound of growth, in spite of the fiscal tightening. The IMF staff repeatedly and explicitly cast doubt on such an outcome, stressing specifically, as in 1991, the fact that the size of the fiscal consolidation was incompatible with growth.

And yet, with the exception of the fiscal targets that were sidelined after October 1993, the performance of the economy with respect to inflation and growth after 1994 proved the government's predictions to be more accurate than those of the IMF staff—albeit with a critical time delay of essentially two years, which can be explained at least partly by the interruption of the reform effort by domestic politics. It is also significant that the 1993 IMF report, for the first time and after related doubts during the previous years, acknowledged that the tight control of personnel costs contributed toward meeting the primary surplus targets of the government's budget.

The IMF frequently recommended that a reduction in government expenditures should take precedence over tax increases. This emphasis on expenditure cuts (later designated as cost control) persisted from 1990 to 2009, which suggests that, with the exception of the 1990–93 administration, successive Greek governments had ignored this message for nearly twenty years. The request to control personnel costs in particular was a consistent feature, and other kinds of expenditures were also mentioned on different occasions. Pension reform and social security reform as well as control of health care expenditures also were perpetual subjects of the recommendations. The sternness of the recommendations varied according to the reforms implemented and planned and intensified with the increasing buildup of imbalances.

The IMF seemed to reflect on similar issues with respect to Greece's participation in the European Exchange Rate Mechanism (EERM) and monetary union, as did the Greek parliament in the debate preceding the ratification of the Maastricht Treaty; it was seen as an opportunity for discipline and reforms. Repeatedly the IMF pointed out the risks of participating in the common currency area for a country with Greece's structural and fiscal imbalances. These were recorded early on, in the form of loosening price competitiveness after EMU accession. During the "good times" though, instead of making the wording harsher, the language actually became more subtle (as the "good times were not taken advantage of"). Developments after 2009 finally confirmed the risks of losing market confidence that the IMF staff report of 1994 had so clearly and bluntly spelled out. Paradoxically, those predictions proved accurate and inaccurate at the same time: although developments after 1994 appeared to discredit the stern assessments of the IMF reports during 1990–93, these critiques were essentially spot-on long term in their descriptions of the dangers to which the country was exposed.[15]

Interestingly, the message regarding "structural reforms" was not consistent. This may be related to the progress shown in some areas after 1990. Prior to then Greece was already considered to be excessively regulated, even given that many other European countries at that time still maintained stringent regulations on their economies. The IMF directors always addressed product market reforms last in their summations, and their comments varied from general references to an emphasis on network industries (a specific selection of these at different times). Only later did specific language focus on the business environment, red tape, and other impediments to economic efficiency.

In 2005 corporate tax rates were reduced, and the IMF directors considered this to be part of the structural reforms then completed and commended the government for this policy. Similarly, the IMF directors (reflecting staff judgment in this matter) commended Greece for structural reforms in product markets in 2007 and praised the related progress made in 2008 and 2009, despite the fact that the aggregate effect of the government's legislative initiatives from 2004 to 2009 was to actually add numerous and significant legal obstacles and institutional uncertainties to doing business. That list is long and includes, for example,

—the introduction of indirect price controls to numerous consumer goods;

—continuation of surreptitious efforts to erode the independence of the Hellenic Competition Commission;

—increases in taxes on mobile communications to the highest level in the EU, in addition to casting legal uncertainty around the licensing of mobile communications base stations;

—establishment of a new licensing law that caused numerous legal problems, especially for productive investments;

—creation of a framework that favored small solar farms (against fiscal and economic rationale but with clear political benefits from providing many licenses to many voters);

—actions to prevent the accumulation of a 20 percent stake in the Hellenic Telecommunications Organization by a private investor, a response that tested the limits of constitutionality and EU law; and

—initiatives that blatantly ignored EU legislation regarding the sale of prefrozen (bake-off) bread.

Unfortunately, numerous other similar instances exist. Clearly, a detailed list of the product market developments during the 2004–09 period does not seem to support the repeated positive recommendations, for three years in a row, by the IMF directors and staff.

It appears that the directors, limited to an assessment of economic facts, did not incorporate into their calculations the pivotal role played by product market regulations in Greece as a manifestation of the collaboration between the authorities and the special interest groups, as described for example in Mitsopoulos and Pelagidis (2009, 2011, 2012). This lack of a political economy assessment suggests that perhaps the IMF directors, as well as many others, were unable to fathom the depth of resistance to dealing honestly with Greece's serious fiscal challenges, such as the inability to reduce excess government expenditure and overstaffing in the public sector—situations directly related to the protection of interest groups and rent-seekers.

In all the IMF reports, the issue of labor markets always took clear precedence over product market reforms and started with a reference to the unit labor cost and cost-competitiveness while, as a second line, wage moderation was almost always demanded. The issue of wage indexation, very relevant to Greece, and the peculiarities of the wage agreements were mentioned in some cases, but the critical role of legislation in the extension of wage agreements and the mediation process that ultimately affects the development of labor costs beyond the minimum wage were never mentioned by the directors—even though in 1991 the new mediation and arbitration system was mentioned by IMF staff, as were sector wage agreements. Yet even that commentary fell short of assessing the pivotal role these factors played in distorting the wage structure in the economy. Also not mentioned by the directors were peculiarities of the wage bargaining process, even though in 2006 the staff detailed the need to decentralize bargaining and address the resistance from the unions on the issue. Over time such peculiarities were incorporated into many different laws (for example, a list of arduous work, weekend pay in seasonal tourism jobs, employment terms in coastal shipping, and technical requirements for certain jobs such as machinery operators). Training, flexible employment terms, employment protection legislation, and job matching were some of the other items occasionally raised by IMF staff. But the inefficiency of the system of registering a new hire or a departure with the authorities was one issue never raised, nor was the inefficiency of the authorities in combating clandestine employment. In general, the IMF reports before 2010 reveal a failure to fully understand how the intricacies of the labor market regulations and the Greek wage bargaining system favored employee representatives and formed a critical juncture in the nexus that redistributed to favored groups the economic rents created by product market regulations, red tape, and the unfavorable business environment.

Finally, as 2009 approached, the balance of payments deficit—15 percent of GDP at the time—started to receive increased attention, as did the accuracy of the statistical data, especially for fiscal developments. Yet, until the end of 2009, these were not seen to have a material impact on the assessment of the sustainability of public finances.

European Union Reports and Decisions before and after Accession of Greece to the Euro Area

When evaluating the decision to admit Greece into the euro area in May 2000, one must bear in mind that by 1999 the macroeconomic variables monitored to assess the convergence required to participate in the EMU had actually improved significantly for Greece. At the same time, governmental policy declarations, as reflected in the national programs presented, were in line with a continuation of the efforts undertaken thus far. The Greek government that submitted the request on March 9, 2000, for reexamination of its convergence situation had a high enough credibility that any impartial observer could assume that the stated goals of the convergence and reform programs did indeed guarantee that the country would be able to join the EMU and ultimately deal with any consequent budgetary and structural challenges.

To be fair, the European Commission's recommendation (EC 2000) and subsequent European Council decision of May 3, 2000, that Greece fulfil the necessary conditions for the adoption of the single currency were issued while the effects of the 1990–93 reforms were still ongoing and the policy stance adopted by the government after 1996 still appeared credible. It would have been humanly impossible at that time to predict the extent to which Greece would fail to address its fiscal and structural challenges in the subsequent decade. Even now, in retrospect, it would have seemed inappropriate if Greece had been excluded on the basis of an anticipated policy failure of the degree that finally occurred. Of course, in a union of many countries that retain national control over key fiscal and structural policies, the occurrence of such a failure seems, with the wisdom of hindsight, to be a likely event—if not within a decade, then surely at some time and not necessarily in a country that initially appears weak. Yet even at the time of its creation, the monetary union was known to be an incomplete project and was seen more as an incremental step in a broader and deeper integration process that would address the possible consequences of exactly such failures. That said, the statements of the first president of the European Central Bank during the 1998–2000 period are most revealing.[16] From the very beginning, in 1998 during the introductory statement to the press conferences following the Governing Council's monetary policy decisions, President Wim Duisenberg expressed the concerns of the Governing Council about the failure of many countries to pursue fiscal policies compatible with the Stability and Growth Pact and explicitly complained that this was also the case with important, large member states. The need to do so and the need to implement growth-enhancing structural reforms in product and labor markets were reiterated with increasing directness. In April 1999 President Duisenberg explicitly stated that monetary policy was not the solution to unemployment that was a consequence of structural factors in inflexible labor, goods, and services markets. Thus, at least from the perspective of the ECB, it is evident that inadequate compliance with the Maastricht criteria was considered a problem—one not limited to a small number of countries but rather broad in scope.

According to the provisions of the Maastricht Treaty, ratified by Greece in 1992, Greece and nine other member states, including Germany and France, were subject to a Council of the EU decision that an excessive deficit had existed since September 1994. The decision followed the approval by the Council, in February of that year, of the recommendations by the EU Monetary Committee on coordinating economic policies and on the conduct of the multilateral surveillance procedures within the Council. This was accompanied by an endorsement of the content and format of the convergence programs and the code of conduct. All these actions have to be placed in the context of the second phase of the EMU, which spanned 1994 to 1998 (European Monetary Institute [EMI] 1996; European Council 2002, 2003; EC 2002, 2003).

The reports by the European Commission and EMI in March 1998 (EMI 1998), according to the process described in EMI (1996)—which formed the basis of the Council's decision on which member states would initially adopt the euro—had resulted in the exclusion of both Sweden and Greece from participation in the final stage of the EMU. The report for Greece accurately described the intensity and duration of the efforts needed to deal with inflation and the fiscal challenges faced by the country, and the vulnerability implied by the high debt level was stressed much more explicitly than it had been in the earlier reports. Those member states assessed in 1998 as not fulfilling the high degree of sustainable convergence required for EMU participation and to maintain the stability and success of the new currency were referred to at the time as "member states with a derogation." This included Greece.

Following the events of 1998, Greece submitted a request on March 9, 2000, for its convergence situation to be reexamined, and in response to that request, the EC prepared a report for the Council in May 2000 (EC 2000). This report concluded that while Greece had fulfilled none of the convergence criteria in 1998, "During the last two years Greece has achieved striking progress towards convergence and the assessment in this report is positive."

The improvement in price stability cited in this report was assumed to be based on sound foundations, and thus despite of the fact that risks were mentioned, the report concluded that "Greece fulfils the criterion on price stability." It stated that "on the latest available figures, the government deficit was brought down from 10.2 percent of GDP in 1995 to 1.6 percent in 1999, below the 3 percent reference value." It also stated that "the debt ratio is expected to continue declining and to fall below 100 percent of GDP in 2001" and that "Greece fulfils the criterion on the government budgetary position." Positive conclusions were also drawn about the exchange rate criteria and legislation regarding the Greek central bank.

Interestingly, comparisons of the development of deficit and inflation numbers in the report evaluated the entire 1990–96 period as one unit instead of analyzing separately the data from 1990 to 1993 and 1994 to 1996. Furthermore, the numbers mentioned for the deficit in 1990 and 1993 included the aggregate numbers, after the addition of the hidden debts accumulated before 1990, and progress was measured against these figures without any elaboration of the impact on such a comparison of the effort of the 1990–93 government to deal with the "hidden" debts and to properly add them to the official debt. The fact that the developments of the 1990–93 and 1994–96 periods were not examined separately in turn implies that the termination of the more determined effort to reduce general government expenditures and stabilize the debt dynamics was not recorded.

The May 2000 report (EC 2000) also mentioned that wages increased moderately in the 1990–93 period and more rapidly thereafter until 1997, driven largely by major increases in public sector wages that had a spill-over effect on the private sector. It also analyzed how renewed modera-tion in wages after 1998 allowed the set criteria to be met. The report weighed the one-time reductions in indirect taxes that reduced inflation at the time of the assessment; these reductions—regarded as permanent— were taken into account in the final assessment of price stability.

The updated convergence program submitted by the Greek govern-ment as a part of the process was extensively commented upon. In view of the government's stated strategy regarding price stability and structural reforms in labor, goods, and capital markets, the report deemed that price stability was sustainable.

It was acknowledged that the drop in interest rates contributed signifi-cantly to reducing the fiscal deficit. Numerous initiatives to raise revenue through structural measures and initiatives to control costs, especially personnel costs and other current expenditures, were also seen as positive, even though they had not contributed to the fiscal consolidation thus far. The surplus of the social security funds was attributed explicitly to the reforms of 1990–92, and all the above were seen to constitute a favor-able starting point for the effort outlined by the updated convergence program. Debt dynamics were in turn assessed in the same context, with the addition of the promised revenue from privatizations.

After Greece's accession to the EMU, the assessments by the EC (EC 2002, 2003, 2004, 2006a) and the Council recommendations published between 2002 and 2008 (European Council 2002, 2003, 2007, 2008) all pointed to the state of public finances in Greece as an urgent and sig-nificant challenge. They singled out the persistently high debt ratio and the obstacles facing the social security system and the business environ-ment, even though they repeatedly also lauded the good progress made on these fronts. The modernization of public administration, tackling of unemployment, and improvement of competition in markets, as well as the performance of the education system, were also assigned the highest priority. Until 2008 the European Council and Commission recommendations often used diplomatic wording that lauded progress even while stressing the need to address the mounting problems, a pattern similar to that of the IMF reports. The broad issues raised were also similar to those raised by the IMF, accurately reflecting the existing problems and a unity in assessments. The more recent evaluations demonstrated a knowledge of the challenges Greece faced that was often more accurate in its details than those in the IMF reports. The same was true concerning the inability of the Greek administration to deal with these challenges. During the same period, the ECB continued to express its firm belief that fiscal consolidation needed to be more resolute in key member states; in some cases the ECB even expressed deep regret or disappointment about the observed developments that had failed to fulfill plans and targets.[17] During 2006, for example, the ECB explicitly stressed that progress in some countries was insufficient and warned that the upswing of the economy should not lead to a procyclical fiscal stance. Similarly, the need for structural reforms and support for the Lisbon Agenda was repeatedly stressed.

In other instances it was forecast by the ECB that Greece's high growth was unlikely to remain above its potential beyond 2004 and that the interplay of rigidities in labor and product markets and the slow development of a knowledge-based society were impeding the increase in labor productivity to levels that would accelerate the catching-up process. And in 2004, based on the Council recommendation made in 2003, the European Commission (EC 2004) pointed out that "the high debt ratio, if not controlled, may put at risk the sustainability of public finances in the longer run when financial pressures stemming from the ageing population are expected to arise." Thus a decade after the 1994 IMF staff report, the European Commission was repeating the same stern and precise warnings.

Essentially, the tone of warnings started to become much sterner by June 2009 with the Council recommendation (European Council 2009), reflecting the European Commission's January recommendation (EC 2009), that Greece "pursue fiscal consolidation in the medium-term and improve the efficiency of primary expenditure, speed up ongoing reforms in tax administration and the budgetary process, reduce the debt-to-GDP ratio, and further proceed with the implementation of the pension reform as rapidly as possible." It was stated in no uncertain terms that Greece's economic and budgetary policies were not in line with the country-specific recommendations issued under the broad economic policy guidelines or the recommendations directed to euro area member states. The administration's low capacity and the challenges this posed to the design and implementation of policies, the loss of price competitiveness, the wage imbalance between the public and private sector, the labor and product market failings, the fiscal imbalances, the issues associated with the social security system, and the vulnerabilities associated with the pressure arising from the pricing of risk were all concisely but comprehensively and accurately spelled out before the document offered a number of detailed, well-targeted, and urgent recommendations. In December 2009 the ECB president expressed in his introductory statement hope that, considering the gravity of the situation, the Greek government would undertake all appropriate and necessary actions.

At the beginning of 2010, the European Council (2010) sent a warning of great importance to the country. Given the limits of its powers, this was probably the most it could do at the time. The subtitle of Recommendation 2010/190/EU from the Council to Greece is telling: "with a view to ending the inconsistency with the broad guidelines of the economic policies in Greece and removing the risk of jeopardising the proper functioning of the economic and monetary union." It reflects the thrust of its contents, the recommendation that "taking into account the institutional weaknesses of the Greek public finances and economy at large, Greece should design and implement, starting as soon as possible in 2010, a bold and comprehensive structural reforms package which goes beyond the measures outlined in the January 2010 update of the stability program. Clear and detailed time plans should be made available for the proposed reforms and followed during implementation" (p. 67).

Interestingly, this recommendation had a precedent: a personal letter by the then president of the European Commission, Jacques Delors, in March 1990, addressed to Greek prime minister Xenophon Zolotas after a crucial election that resulted in the formation of a caretaker administration with virtually no capacity for strong governance.[18] The 2010 recommendation, however, came at a time when a very recently elected Greek government had a comfortable majority in the parliament and arguably had a stronger mandate and political capacity to deliver on its commitments and obligations.

This historical recurrence is not the only one that indicates the similarities between the developments of the 1990–93 period and those after 2010. In 1990 Greece, unable to cover current government budget expenditures, had asked for and received a loan from the very reluctant European Community. The loan was secured only with a contractual undertaking to implement a broad program of structural reforms and fiscal consolidation measures. This loan, together with the resolute implementation of the program by the Greek government at the time, succeeded in restoring the confidence of financial markets in the country, and thus gradually these markets became accessible again to the government. This, together with the use of financial engineering tools, made it possible for the country to avoid seeking assistance from the IMF. It is noteworthy that in his inaugural parliamentary speech in April 1990, the incoming prime minister Mitsotakis responded to opposition complaints about the harshness of his proposed agenda for structural reforms and fiscal consolidation by stating that the country should avoid at all costs seeking assistance from the IMF, since the fund would impose even harsher terms, and that the strategy he proposed was the only way to avoid such an undesirable scenario for Greece.

2

The Depression of the Century
Prejudice and Misguided Policies

This chapter investigates the extent to which the success of the "internal devaluation" (reduction of incomes and asset prices) strategy depended not only on quantitative aspects of the initiatives but also on qualitative implementation of those policy initiatives. While the apparent success of labor market reforms after 2012—that is, the stabilization and even gradual increase in employment levels after the large decline of the 2010–12 period—is noted, so are two other facts. First, as a result of widespread self-employment in Greece, the potential benefits of reducing private sector wage costs were limited, even before the adjustment program began. This is particularly obvious when the benefits of reducing administrative costs and deregulating markets are taken into account. Second, forcing internal devaluation predominantly onto the private sector actually worsened the balance between the tax base and the government sector, with the latter expecting to be able to pay pensions and public sector wages from the taxes levied on the former. A disproportional focus on revenue increases further exacerbated the impact of this misguided approach.

Analysis of developments in the Greek financial sector illuminates how internal devaluation was pushed predominantly onto the private sector, not only as a result of policies that favored tax increases over cost cutting but also due to strategic decisions such as the imposition of private sector involvement (PSI), increasing uncertainty about the European prospects of the country, and more recent intimations of a "bail-in" for private deposits.[1] Developments in the financial sector demonstrate not only the impressive resilience of the Greek financial system, with the unquestionable support of the Eurosystem, but also how policymakers allowed the fiscal crisis of the country to gradually entangle the private sector in a full-blown, textbook-style liquidity crisis, with grave and unnecessary implications for economic activity and employment.

Sectoral Developments

The decline in economic activity in various sectors of Greek industry (manufacturing plus mining and energy) continued during 2012, with more sectors exhibiting lower activity, as measured by the Eurostat index, and with the declines in each sector increasing in absolute value (table 2-1). Among the hardest hit were textiles, apparel, leather, and furniture, sectors that had been declining for many years as a result of both increasing global competition from other countries with lower production costs and an inability to move up the value chain. Some of the sectors listed in table 2-1 also are affected by the activities of state-owned, or formerly state-owned, companies (for example, manufacture of transport equipment); face severe institutional impediments; or are hampered by declining government investment in ICT infrastructure.[2] The slow-down in economic restructuring arising from institutional uncertainty also had an impact on some sectors, such as the manufacture of computers, electronics, and optical products.

On the other hand, utilities (such as electricity, gas, water, and sewage treatment) have benefited, for example, from the expansion of the natural gas supply network and the resulting increase in consumption—or from similar developments. In other cases, such as government-controlled utilities, turnover has directly benefited from administratively set price increases. Domestic sectors with competitive, export-oriented private companies that manage to keep up with international markets, such as refineries and metal producers, were among the strongest performers. This is also true of the food industry, which traditionally has been an innovative and strong performer in Greece.

Table 2-2 shows the annual gross employee earnings for 2009 by economic activity according to NACE Rev. 2.[3] A comparison with ten other European countries for which these data are available yields some interesting findings. First, the average gross employee earnings in the Greek "accommodation and food services" sector are notable in 2009 for how much they exceeded the average of the other countries. Though the 2009 data do not reflect the reality after 2012, numerous provisions of related legislation ensured that employee compensation in this sector was very generous (and in many ways remains so). For example,

Table 2-1. *Industrial Production per Sector, 2008–12*

Percent change

Industry production index – monthly data (2005 = 100) (NACE Rev. 2) [sts_inpr_m]	Change from 12-2008 to 12-2012
Manufacture of other transport equipment	−72.8
Manufacture of computer, electronic, and optical products	−67.9
Manufacture of furniture	−67.2
Manufacture of motor vehicles, trailers, and semi-trailers	−65.6
Manufacture of leather and related products	−64.0
Manufacture of wearing apparel	−56.7
Manufacture of other nonmetallic mineral products	−54.8
Manufacture of textiles	−54.7
Printing and reproduction of recorded media	−51.8
Repair and installation of machinery and equipment	−45.9
Manufacture of beverages	−33.7
Other manufacturing	−32.6
Manufacture of machinery and equipment n.e.c.	−31.8
Manufacture of tobacco products	−29.4
Manufacture of fabricated metal products, except machinery and equipment	−28.1
Manufacture of paper and paper products	−24.3
Manufacture of electrical equipment	−24.3
Electricity, gas, steam, and air conditioning supply	−23.5
Mining and quarrying	−17.0
Manufacture of rubber and plastic products	−15.7
Manufacture of chemicals and chemical products	−8.0
Manufacture of basic pharmaceutical products and pharmaceutical preparations	−7.7
Manufacture of basic metals	−7.6
Manufacture of food products	−7.5
Water collection, treatment, and supply	−6.7
Manufacture of wood and of products of wood and cork, except furniture; manufacture of articles of straw and plaiting materials	−5.2
Manufacture of coke and refined petroleum products	13.5

Source: Eurostat, "Production in Industry—Monthly Data," NACE Rev. 2 [sts_inpr_m] (http://epp.eurostat. ec.europa.eu/portal/page/portal/statistics/search_database).

legislation required seasonal staff in the accommodation sector to be paid a surcharge of almost 100 percent if they worked on Saturdays or Sundays (something absolutely normal for the hotel industry in the summer). Still, while the sector wage agreements in the hotel business used to be very generous to employees in many other ways, this changed

Table 2-2. *Annual Gross Employee Earnings by Economic Activity, 2009*
Units as indicated

Economic activity	Thousands of 2009 euros, Greece	Greece vs. average of 10 countries (percent higher or lower)[a]
Accommodation and food service activities	37.5	+87.1
Electricity, gas, steam, and air conditioning supply	55.7	+49.0
Real estate activities	37.2	+39.2
Water supply; sewerage, waste management, and remediation activities	32.6	+31.8
Transportation and storage	33.9	+24.6
Administrative and support service activities	23.6	+11.0
Manufacturing	26.0	+7.5
Business economy	29.2	+5.7
Information and communication	36.9	+1.9
Education	27.9	−1.5
Wholesale and retail trade; repair of motor vehicles and motorcycles	24.2	−2.2
Financial and insurance activities	36.0	−4.0
Arts, entertainment and recreation	20.7	−5.6
Human health and social work activities	23.6	−6.0
Other service activities	20.0	−7.0
Professional, scientific, and technical activities	28.1	−14.4
Mining and quarrying	25.0	−14.7
Construction	21.7	−15.9

Source: Eurostat database (http://epp.eurostat.ec.europa.eu/portal/page/portal/statistics/search_database).
a. Countries with available data are Ireland (not all sectors), Greece, Spain, Latvia, Malta, Netherlands, Portugal, Slovakia, Finland, and Sweden.

after the labor market reforms of 2012. Recently businesses in this sector and the respective unions have concluded a wage agreement with much more modest provisions, resulting in a significant fall in average wages (according to recent official data from the IKA, the main private sector social security fund), even though the aforementioned surcharges still apply.[4] Another illustrative example is the 17 percent tip surcharge for servers added by law to the price of served food and drinks. Such examples support the observation that the annual gross earnings in the accommodation and food services sector for 2009 were very high by international standards.[5]

A further observation is that in key sectors dominated by large state-owned (or state-controlled) enterprises, such as energy and water utilities, wages are not only relatively high compared to the other sectors of the economy but also when compared to the average employee earnings of the ten European countries for which data are available. Finally, other sectors in which earnings appear high when compared to other countries, such as transport and storage, were also subject, at least in 2009, to regulation providing for mandatory minimum fees. It must be kept in mind though that these minimum fees have since been abolished in many cases (an indicative example is road haulage services), and thus employee earnings in the transport and storage sector may have changed substantially after 2009. Overall, gross earnings in the manufacturing sector in 2009 exceeded by about 7.5 percent the average of the ten countries serving as a basis for comparison. For the business economy as a whole (which, however, includes some large state-controlled companies known for large salaries), the difference in 2009 was about 5 percent. Since in both cases the average includes the high wages in state-owned or state-subsidized industries, this was not a particularly significant difference.

Within the industrial sector, the highest labor costs per employee, which beyond wages also include other forms of compensation and overtime or night-shift surcharges, are basically found in industries characterized by strong export activity (refineries, basic metal processing), a significant presence of state-owned companies (electricity production, water supply and sewerage, manufacture of transport equipment), or a tradition of generous wages for their employees, for various reasons (see table 2-3). On the other hand, the lowest labor costs are observed in industries facing challenges, such as furniture, leather products, and apparel manufacturing.

As shown in figure 2-1, a significant number of sectors had high costs per employee in 2009 and a production index that demonstrated above-average resilience from 2008 until 2012. It should be noted that in some sectors, such as refining, the strong export performance of the sector suggests that high labor costs were in line with the good financial performance of the companies. In other sectors with a large presence of state-controlled companies, such as energy and water utilities, their effective monopoly over the market implied a more resilient performance and enabled them to support higher costs per employee. Furthermore, figure 2-2 suggests that, at least until 2009, higher cost per employee in a sector was positively related to the minimum compensation provided for a benchmark employee by the sector wage agreement when compared to the national minimum set by the collective minimum national wage agreement, thus providing evidence that these sector agreements indeed often increased wages above the national averages as binding constraints.

Table 2-3. *Labor Cost per Employee, by Industry, 2009*

Thousands of euros

Industry	Labor cost per employee FTE[a]
Manufacture of coke and refined petroleum products	87.2
Manufacture of tobacco products	51.5
Electricity, gas, steam, and air conditioning supply	49.3
Water supply; sewerage, waste management, and remediation activities	49.2
Manufacture of other transport equipment	43.4
Manufacture of beverages	42.5
Mining and quarrying	34.9
Printing and reproduction of recorded media	34.7
Manufacture of basic metals	33.1
Manufacture of other nonmetallic mineral products	32.3
Manufacture of basic pharmaceutical products and pharmaceutical preparations	31.3
Manufacture of chemicals and chemical products	31.1
Manufacture of paper and paper products	29.1
Manufacture of electrical equipment	27.6
Manufacture of textiles	26.3
Manufacture of food products	25.9
Manufacture of rubber and plastic products	25.5
Manufacture of motor vehicles, trailers, and semi-trailers	25.4
Manufacture of computer, electronic, and optical products	24.9
Manufacture of fabricated metal products, except machinery and equipment	24.6
Manufacture of machinery and equipment n.e.c.	23.8
Repair and installation of machinery and equipment	22.6
Manufacture of furniture	22.4
Manufacture of leather and related products	22.3
Manufacture of wood and of products of wood and cork, except furniture; manufacture of articles of straw and plaiting materials	21.3
Manufacture of wearing apparel	20.8
Other manufacturing	20.1
Manufacturing	28.4

Source: Eurostat, "Annual Detailed Enterprise Statistics for Industry, Greece," NACE Rev. 2, B-E [sbs_na_ind_r2] (http://epp.eurostat.ec.europa.eu/portal/page/portal/statistics/search_database).

a. FTE, full-time equivalent.

Figure 2-1. *Cost per Employee and Resilience of Production Index*

Production index (percent change 12-2008 to 12-2012)

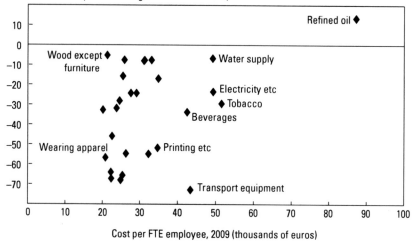

Cost per FTE employee, 2009 (thousands of euros)

Source: Eurostat database (http://epp.eurostat.ec.europa.eu/portal/page/portal/statistics/search_database).

Figure 2-2. *Average Cost per Employee and Minimum Daily Wage per Sector Agreement, 2009*[a]

Average cost (thousands of euros)

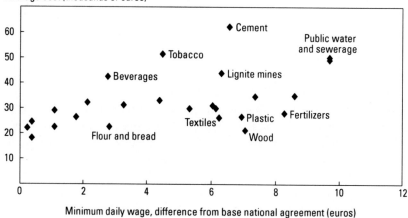

Minimum daily wage, difference from base national agreement (euros)

Source: Authors' calculations based on data from the Organization of Mediation and Arbitration (www.omed. gr) and Eurostat (http://epp.eurostat.ec.europa.eu/portal/page/portal/statistics/search_database).
a. Analysis of 2009 collective sector (or professional group) agreement (posted by OMED) for benchmark nonmarried employee with three years' service at the same employer and its difference from the national minimum wage agreement of the year and the comparison of the difference with the cost of an employee for the sector (or a sector with a large dependence on the professional group), as provided by Eurostat for 2009.

Table 2-4. *Labor Cost Index Evolution per Sector, 2008–12*

Percent change

Sector	2008 Q1/ 2000 Q1	2011 Q1/ 2008 Q1	2012 Q1/ 2008 Q1
Electricity, gas, steam, and air conditioning supply	135.7	12.2	−28.2
Water supply; sewerage, waste management, and remediation activities	97.2	−8.5	−19.7
Professional, scientific, and technical activities	76.9	3.0	−1.4
Administrative and support service activities	74.3	−1.4	−7.2
Public administration and defense; compulsory social security	68.5	−15.5	−29.3
Other service activities	54.7	-6.9	−13.4
Education	53.4	−10.4	−24.0
Human health and social work activities	50.5	−19.0	−22.8
Arts, entertainment, and recreation	45.8	−15.8	−18.9
Information and communication	44.1	4.2	4.0
Real estate activities	43.9	17.2	11.5
Transportation and storage	41.7	2.1	−11.9
Accommodation and food service activities	33.0	−25.0	−20.6
Wholesale and retail trade; repair of motor vehicles and motorcycles	26.1	12.9	13.4
Construction	25.6	1.5	−7.9
Mining and quarrying	23.1	8.5	10.0
Manufacturing	21.2	2.6	−3.0
Financial and insurance activities	16.4	3.0	−3.6

Source: Eurostat.

Table 2-4 shows how some sectors, such as electricity and gas supply, posted the largest labor cost index increases from 2000 until 2008. In particular, the sectors with significant state influence, such as electricity and gas supply and water and sewerage, stand out not only for their large labor cost increases during the 2000–08 period but also for the fact that until 2011 they seemed rather shielded from labor cost reductions. In those sectors labor cost reductions appeared on a noteworthy scale only in 2012. The other sectors with large labor cost increases from 2000 to 2008 were also strongly influenced by government regulations related to remuneration (professional services) or directly related to the state (public administration). Manufacturing, on the other hand, stands out for its very modest increase in labor cost index during the 2000–08 period.

Table 2-5 shows in which Greek manufacturing sectors during 2009 the personnel cost significantly exceeded the EU-27 average, as a percentage

Table 2-5. *Personnel Costs as Percent of Turnover and Cost per Employee*

Units as indicated

Sector	Personnel cost (percent of turnover or gross premium written), Greece	Greece vs. EU-27 average (percent higher or lower)[b]	Labor cost per employee FTE[c] (thousands of euros)
Electricity, gas, steam and air conditioning supply	. . .[a]	. . .[a]	49.3
Manufacture of coke and refined petroleum products	3.3	1.0	87.2
Manufacture of tobacco products	17.0	11.6	51.5
Water supply; sewerage, waste management, and remediation activities	55.2	34.7	49.2
Manufacture of other transport equipment	48.9	27.6	43.4
Manufacture of beverages	18.7	6.9	42.5
Mining and quarrying	25.7	14.5	34.9
Printing and reproduction of recorded media	38.2	11.1	34.7
Manufacture of basic metals	14.4	1.1	33.1
Manufacture of other non-metallic mineral products	22.4	1.9	32.3
Manufacture of basic pharmaceutical products and pharmaceutical preparations	17.2	2.7	31.3
Manufacture of chemicals and chemical products	15.6	1.6	31.1
Manufacture of paper and paper products	20.2	3.8	29.1
Manufacture of electrical equipment	16.4	−5.7	27.6
Manufacture of textiles	27.6	4.8	26.3
Manufacturing of food products	15.0	2.8	25.9
Manufacture of rubber and plastic products	21.3	0.4	25.5
Manufacture of motor vehicles, trailers, and semi-trailers	34.8	20.1	25.4
Manufacture of computer, electronic, and optical products	25.6	7.2	24.9
Manufacture of fabricated metal products, except machinery and equipment	20.6	−4.2	24.6
Manufacture of machinery and equipment n.e.c.	29.0	5.7	23.8
Repair and installation of machinery and equipment	29.1	0.6	22.6

(*continued*)

Table 2-5 (*continued*)

Sector	Personnel cost (percent of turnover or gross premium written), Greece	Greece vs. EU-27 average (percent higher or lower)[b]	Labor cost per employee FTE[c] (thousands of euros)
Manufacture of furniture	30.9	6.4	22.4
Manufacture of leather and related products	25.0	6.7	22.3
Manufacture of wood and of products of wood and cork, except furniture; manufacture of articles of straw and plaiting materials	19.2	0.6	21.3
Manufacture of wearing apparel	22.0	1.8	20.8
Other manufacturing	24.0	0.8	20.1
Manufacturing	16.2	−0.8	28.4

Source: Eurostat, "Annual Detailed Enterprise Statistics for Industry," NACE Rev. 2, B-E [sbs_na_ind_r2] (http://epp.eurostat.ec.europa.eu/portal/page/portal/statistics/search_database).
a. Not available for Greece.
b. By percent of turnover.
c. FTE = full-time equivalent.

of turnover or gross premiums. Apart from the conspicuous absence of data for the sector of electricity supply, the sectors that differ the most from the European average are those where the state exerts significant influence (water supply and sewerage, manufacture of transport equipment) or have certain peculiarities (such as tobacco production, which has a tradition of paying high wages to workers, and printing and media, which legislation has granted numerous privileges thanks to their strong ties to the political elite). On the other hand, refining and the manufacture of basic metals seem to have a very reasonable labor cost structure when compared to other countries, in spite of both their relatively high per employee compensation and strong export performance that some sectors (for example, metals) still exhibited at the time. Overall, this exposition strongly suggests that one should use the average data (such as unit labor cost for the whole economy) with great caution and proceed with the careful investigation of more detailed data before formulating strong policy recommendations with respect to the significance of labor costs for the Greek economy—in particular regarding the competitiveness of sectors that are expected to spearhead an export-led recovery. The available evidence strongly suggests that all the analyses that link the current crisis simply to the evolution of unit labor cost (and all its variants or

Figure 2-3. *Employment and Unemployment, 1998–2013*

Thousands of individuals

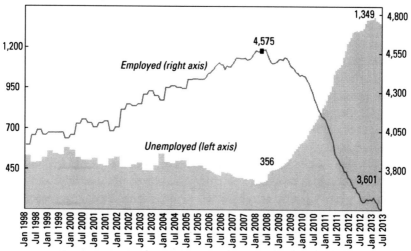

Sources: EL.STAT (http://tinyurl.com/nuqy96t) and Eurostat (http://epp.eurostat.ec.europa.eu/portal/page/portal/statistics/search_database).

contributing parts) should be evaluated carefully given the very diverse cost composition of each separate sector.

Developments in Employment, Wages, Earnings, and Labor Cost

Our breakdown of labor costs by sector reveals a much more complex reality than assumed by the proponents of the "unconditional internal devaluation." In this section we examine the trends in the relevant measures of labor costs and employment levels. Such a complete analysis is necessary to accurately document which policies can indeed help to improve the performance of the Greek labor market.

Employment. Starting out from a relatively low employment-to-population ratio, the Greek economy demonstrated a significant loss of employment since the onset of the "Greek crisis." Figure 2-3 illustrates the opposing trends in employment and unemployment from 2011 through 2013, with a net loss of about 1 million jobs since the onset of the crisis and a concurrent increase in the number of the unemployed also by about a million. The latter number includes youth newly entering the workforce who cannot find jobs while the former number includes workers retiring from the public sector.

Again, a sectoral breakdown provides important insights. Comparing data (table 2-6) for the third quarter of each year since 2008, one can see how employment in public administration and in sectors primarily associated with state-owned companies (electricity generation and distribution, water and sewerage) demonstrated resilience until 2011 and started to decline significantly only during 2012. The decline in employment in public administration was due to retirement, not layoffs, as reflected in the increasing number of public sector pensioners, according to official data. On the other hand, the private sector activity, excluding construction, was shedding jobs at a rate exceeding 10 percent in 2011; by 2012 there had been a cumulative 20 percent loss of jobs since 2008. Thus, not only did the private sector start losing jobs much earlier than both the public sector and companies in sectors with some public control, but even when the overall public sector started to move employees into retirement in 2012, net layoffs in the private sector still increased faster, basically doubling again during 2012. The situation in the construction sector was even more severe, with the sector shedding half its jobs since the onset of the crisis as a result of the serious policy errors concerning the real estate market and the loss of financing for large infrastructure projects.

Loss of employment is also observed among the self-employed, mainly because of tax measures and increases in the fixed contributions, which caused many low-income self-employed to discontinue their registration with the tax authorities, as the high fixed cost of registration was no longer sustainable with their diminished occasional or low income. In spite of this, the ratio of self-employed to total population in Greece remains significantly above the euro area average. On the other hand, the shrinking ratio of employees to total population, which already was significantly below the euro area average before the crisis, has declined further and faster. Thus all gains in employment to population, and especially in the employees-to-population ratio, that had been achieved since 1999 were essentially lost (Figures 2-4 and 2-5).

Wages and Earnings. The low level of salaried employment is one of the principal reasons why the compensation of employees in the total economy is so low in Greece; the other reason is the low level of salaries. Again, the decline in the compensation of employees to GDP, in spite of its already low levels, since the onset of the crisis is clearly documented and is in line with the stated policy objective of internal devaluation (figure 2-6).

A comparison of the ratio of employee compensation to GDP for those employed in corporations (figure 2-7) reveals that, during the 2010–12

Table 2-6. *Employment per Sector, Greece, 2008–12*

Units as indicated

Employment	Thousands employed, Q3					Change in number employed (thousands)			Percent change	
	2008	2009	2010	2011	2012	2008–11	2008–12		2008–11	2008–12
All activities	**4,589.8**	**4,540.1**	**4,402.9**	**4,079.3**	**3,739.0**	**–510.5**	**–850.8**		**–11.1**	**–18.5**
Agriculture	513.9	514.9	515.9	516.9	517.9	3.0	4.0		0.6	0.8
Trade, manufacturing, accommodation and food, professional activities, transportation and storage, financial services, ICT, support activities, arts, mining, real estate, other activities, households, media and communications	2,688.9	2,634.3	2,545.0	2,374.6	2,156.3	–314.3	–532.6		–11.7	–19.8
Public administration, defense, education, health and social work, water supply and sewerage, electricity, gas and A/C production and supply	986.8	983.5	987.2	958.9	886.6	–27.9	–100.2		-2.8	–10.2
Construction	398.8	376.9	319.4	241.8	204.8	–157.0	–194.0		–39.4	–48.6

Source: ELSTAT–Eurostat, "Employment—Greece" NACE 2 (http://tinyurl.com/octrdns) and Eurostat (http://epp.eurostat.ec.europa.eu/portal/page/portal/statistics/search_database).

Figure 2-4. *Self-employed to Total Population, Euro Area 18 versus Greece, 1999–2013*

Percent

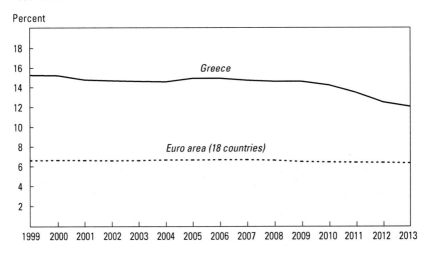

Source: European Commission, AMECO database (NETN-NWTN)/NPTD (http://ec.europa.eu/economy_finance/ameco/user/serie/SelectSerie.cfm).

Figure 2-5. *Employees to Total Population, Euro Area 18 versus Greece, 1999–2013*

Percent

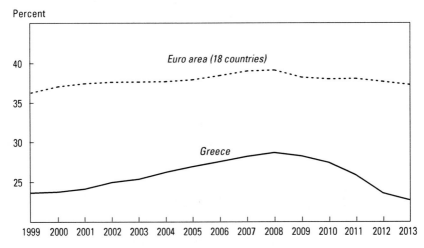

Source: European Commission, AMECO database, NWTD/NPTD (http://ec.europa.eu/economy_finance/ameco/user/serie/SelectSerie.cfm).

Figure 2-6. *Compensation of Employees, Total Economy, to GDP, Euro Area 18 versus Greece, 1999–2013*

Percent

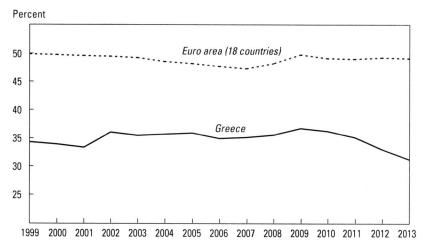

Source: European Commission, AMECO database, UWCD/UVGD (http://ec.europa.eu/economy_finance/ameco/user/serie/SelectSerie.cfm).

Figure 2-7. *Compensation of Employees, Corporations, to GDP, Euro Area 18 versus Greece, 1999–2013*

Percent

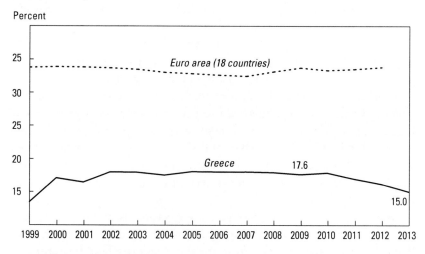

Source: European Commission, AMECO database, UWCC/UVGD (http://ec.europa.eu/economy_finance/ameco/user/serie/SelectSerie.cfm).

Figure 2-8. *Compensation of Employees, Total Economy minus Corporations, to GDP, Euro Area 18 versus Greece, 1999–2013*

Percent

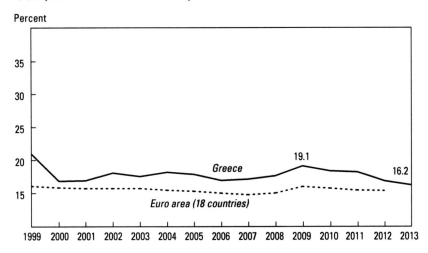

Source: European Commission, AMECO database (UWCD-UWCC)/UVGD (http://ec.europa.eu/economy_finance/ameco/user/serie/SelectSerie.cfm).

period at least, the decline in employee compensation occurred proportionally in the corporate-private sector and in the parts of the economy that exclude the corporate sector and that mainly include the general government (figure 2-8), in spite of the fact that the former was already low by European standards and the latter high.

This finding accords with the widely held belief that public sector employees (the main group of employees not added to the corporate sector by AMECO) were both numerous and highly paid in Greece and that they were, at least until 2013, well shielded by policymakers from the impact of the crisis in comparison to private sector employees. This is further corroborated by an assessment of Greece's progress with its Second Economic Adjustment Program (EC 2013c, table B2), which states that in 2013 compensation per employee in the general government was still over 50 percent higher than the average compensation per employee in the private sector.

As explained earlier, employee compensation is a product of two variables, the number of employees and the amount of compensation. Regarding the latter, the data from the social security fund for most private sector employees (IKA) reveal how the downward adjustment of wages (that is, gross wages, including social security contributions of the employee but not those of the employer, and excluding bonuses, overtime, and other payments, including payments in kind) started to accelerate only during 2012 (Figure 2-9). The data also show how the bulk of the adjustment until 2012 was essentially realized by the decline in employment (figure 2-10).

The employment considered here excludes construction sites, which have a separate legal status. For the construction sector a significant part of the drop in employment comes from the virtual freeze in construction activity, reflected in the decline in the number of employees on construction sites from 120,000 in January 2009 to less than 40,000 in January 2012. The fact that until early 2012 the bulk of the adjustment in employee compensation in the private sector—excluding construction— seems to have occurred via the reduction of employment, while regular earnings remained broadly stable, can be attributed to the fact that useful changes in the labor laws were enacted only since 2012. These include the introduction of a reduced minimum wage and, more important, an increased flexibility to set wages above the minimum without the constraints of earlier sectoral and professional wage agreements.

The Organization of Mediation and Arbitration (OMED) provides an analysis of the sectoral wage agreements that reveals the extent to which additional agreements in each separate sector and profession exceeded the national minimum wage set through the national wage agreement. Based on the organization's 2009 data, figure 2-2 suggests a positive correlation between average cost per employee and minimum wage, and it appears that the subsequent change in these laws made it possible to reduce wage costs in many industries, an outcome reflected in the records of the IKA since 2012. An illustrative example is the rapid and sizeable decrease in hotel industry wages only since 2012.

Eurostat data (figure 2-11) show how nonwage labor compensation fell rapidly and faster than wages and salaries after 2010 as companies sought to reduce labor costs in the context of the constraints that made it impossible to lower regular wages. Reduction in overtime, shutting down production lines on weekends and terminating night shifts for which surcharges have to be paid, ending bonuses and profit-sharing for employees, and stopping practices such as the distribution of food coupons and the provision of cell phones, company cars, or company credit cards all helped to trim nonwage labor costs drastically in the period from the start of the crisis until early 2012.

Figure 2-9. *Average Gross Wage per Day, Regular Earnings, Enterprises except Construction Sites, 2010–13*

Percent change from same month, previous year

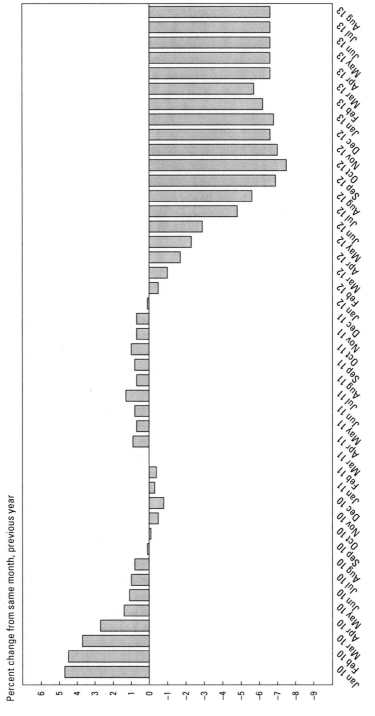

Source: IKA (www.ika.gr/gr/infopages/stats/stat_report.cfm).

Figure 2-10. *Change in Number Employed by Enterprises except Construction Sites, 2010–13*

Percent change from same month, previous year

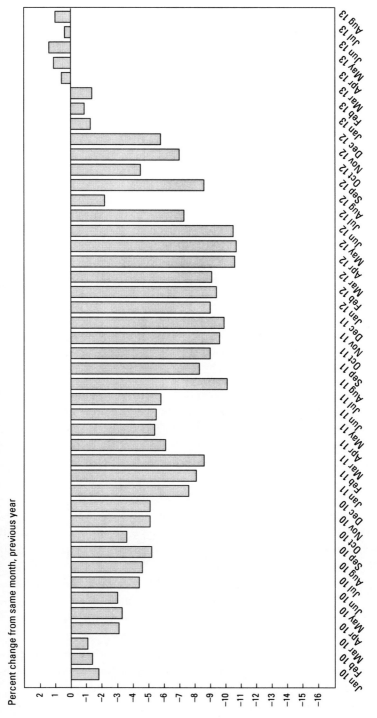

Source: IKA (www.ika.gr/gr/infopages/stats/stat_report.cfm).

Figure 2-11. *Labor Cost Indexes, Market Economy, Greece, 2008–12*

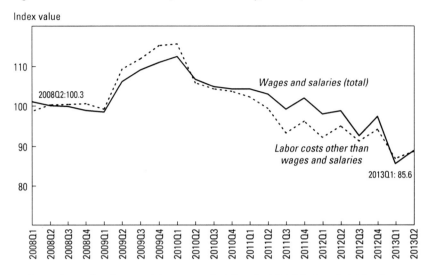

Source: Eurostat (http://epp.eurostat.ec.europa.eu/portal/page/portal/statistics/search_database).

The preceding analysis demonstrates that the measures of labor cost and competitiveness usually cited by researchers examining Greece must always be scrutinized carefully. Percentage changes in labor cost indexes with respect to some arbitrarily selected base year (for example, the year of Greece's accession to the euro area) rarely indicate that the absolute level of wages and the total compensation of employees in Greece remained well below European averages even before the onset of the crisis. Furthermore, after the reductions of the past three to four years, they are now actually even lower. In particular, Eurostat data reveal that the (taxable) gross income per employee in all sectors fell by over 14 percent from 2009 until 2013 (figure 2-12). One has to stress here that this relates only to those who are still employed, as those who became unemployed during this period are not included any more in this statistic. By 2013 nominal compensation per employee in Greece had fallen to 46 percent below the euro area average. In addition, one must remember that wages in competitive, tradable sectors of the economy, such as food and manufacturing, were and are much lower than those in sectors that have the benefit of government protection from competition, such as electricity production or water utilities (nontradable sectors) or government wages (EC 2013c), and are even lower when compared respectively with European averages.

Figure 2-12. *Nominal Compensation per Employee, Total Economy, 2000–13*

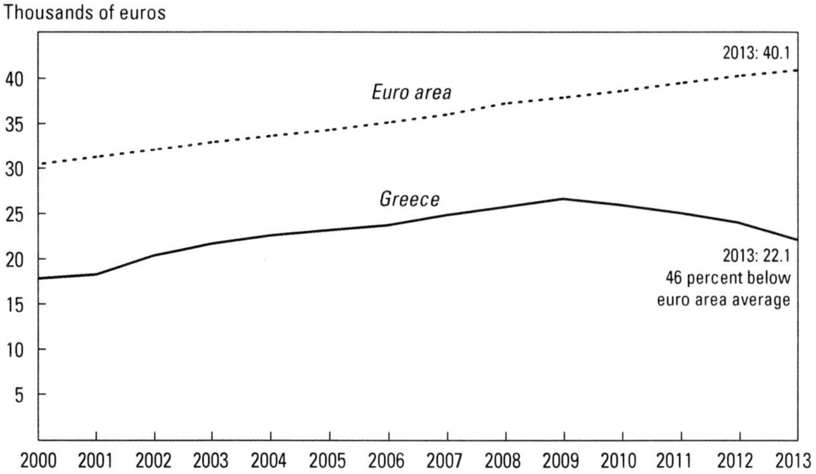

Thousands of euros

Source: European Commission, AMECO database, HWCDW (http://ec.europa.eu/economy_finance/ameco/user/serie/SelectSerie.cfm).

It has to be stressed, though, that in the long-run, changes in labor market regulations implemented after 2012, and the impact they have already had on that market, suggest that an anticipated recovery should be much richer in jobs when compared with the previous period of rapid growth.

Labor Cost Indexes. While all indexes of labor cost and of competitiveness somehow reflect the combined effect of the developments discussed above (see figure 2-13), these complex indexes—which are often ratios of ratios—often fail to indicate that the compensation per employee in Greece is now more than 45 percent below the euro area average. Furthermore, such indexes sometimes use data for the aggregate economy, sometimes only for the business economy, sometimes wages only, and sometimes total compensation per employee. They also vary across parameters, such as the use of nominal or real values. In all these cases, the consequence is different results, and thus the range and nature of all separate variables included in these indexes must be carefully considered and analyzed before strong conclusions can be drawn.

In addition, the averages do not convey the fact that labor costs are less important for some sectors than for others. For example, the excise tax on energy increased by an average of about 20 percent since 2008, and this combined with increases in energy prices during the same period

Figure 2-13. *Real Unit Labor Cost, Total Economy, Performance Relative to the Rest of Former EU-15, 2000–13*

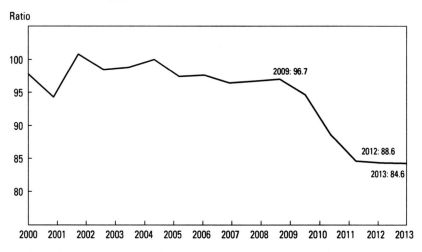

Source: European Commission, AMECO database, QLCDQ (http://ec.europa.eu/economy_finance/ameco/user/serie/SelectSerie.cfm).

meant that the energy-intensive branches of industry in Greece ended up paying as much as 80 percent more for energy than similar companies in other major euro area and EU countries.[6] So if the cumulative effect of the excise tax–induced cost increases were to be compensated for, labor costs would have to be cut by as much as 80 percent in industries such as steel mills and aluminum smelters where energy constitutes up to 50 percent of all costs and labor often as little as 15 percent of all costs. Even if such energy-intensive sectors represent the extremes, it is still true that as a result of stringent labor market regulation and high taxation of salaried labor, the Greek economy had shifted the use of inputs away from wage-earning employment and toward self-employment and more intense use of capital. Thus employee compensation by corporations as a percentage of GDP gradually became significantly lower in Greece than in other euro area countries even while public employee compensation, again as a percentage of GDP, rose to above average.

The significant sectoral variations in labor cost levels and the evolution of the indexes further support the assertion that the internal devaluation of incomes following the first three years of implementation of the conditionality program focused predominantly on the private sector of the economy, where the labor cost of salaried employment was much less significant to the competitiveness of the economy than it would have been in an average euro area country. On the other hand, the above-average public sector labor costs, which were clearly a much larger problem, were reduced relatively late in the process and, proportionally, to a lesser degree than in the private sector. Thus in 2013 the per capita compensation in the general government still exceeded private sector compensation by over 50 percent, and this does not reflect the fact that the fall in employment in the private sector was predominantly the result of layoffs, while in the public sector it was mainly the result of retirement schemes—a development that cemented the proportionally stronger internal devaluation of the private sector.

In the final analysis, the foregoing evidence suggests that the way internal devaluation was implemented in Greece contributed less to the improvement of cost competitiveness than would have been the case in the average euro area country. Furthermore, the focus of internal devaluation on the earnings and the number of private sector employees had the effect of reducing one of the most lucrative sources of the country's tax revenue and social security contributions. This in turn minimized any potentially beneficial impact on the state of public finances. This situation is even more striking when one considers that precrisis, Greece really stood out as the euro area member with the lowest ratio of private sector wages to GDP and the highest estimated administrative cost to GDP (figure 2-14). Thus Greece was the country that had the smallest potential for improving cost-competitiveness through reduction of private sector wage costs and the greatest potential to improve cost-competitiveness by reducing red tape and administrative costs. With respect to the latter, it should be stressed that a critical mass of reforms is now slowly accumulating that should gradually support a solid recovery. Numerous examples range from the licensing process for businesses to cruise-ship homeporting.

Public Finances

Examination of the structure of Greek general government revenue up to 2010 clearly confirms some salient features of the Greek fiscal situation at the time the conditionality program was adopted and into the first year of its implementation (see EC 2012b). For example, a deficit in tax revenue of about 5 percent of GDP persisted until the start of the crisis. This was a result of a shortfall of direct taxes (figure 2-15), and not of a shortfall in indirect taxes, which remained, as a percentage of GDP, equal to European averages (figure 2-16), despite the fact that consumption formed a larger share of GDP in Greece than in the other European countries

Figure 2-14. *Private Sector Gross Wages and Salaries versus Administrative Cost as a Percent of GDP, European Countries, 2003*

Percent of GDP

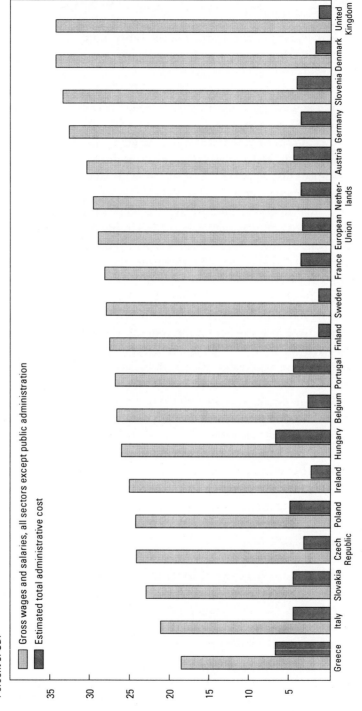

Source: Eurostat (gross wages and salaries); 2005 Kox Report for European Commission (administrative cost).

Figure 2-15. *Direct Taxes, 1995–2011*

Percent of GDP

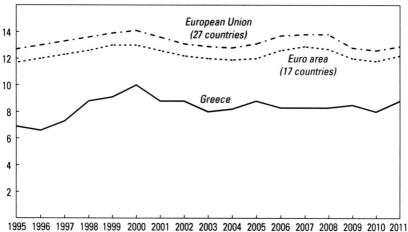

Source: European Commission, Tax Database (http://tinyurl.com/6l2wvw).

Figure 2-16. *Indirect Taxes, 1996–2011*

Percent of GDP

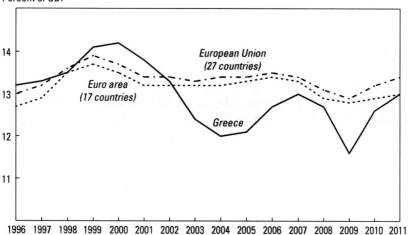

Source: European Commission, Tax Database (http://tinyurl.com/6l2wvw).

Figure 2-17. *Final Consumption Expenditure to GDP, Current Prices, 2000–12*

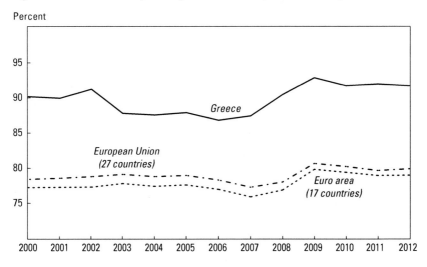

Source: Eurostat (http://epp.eurostat.ec.europa.eu/portal/page/portal/statistics/search_database).

(figure 2-17); the take of value added tax (VAT) and other indirect taxes should therefore have been larger, and the related tax evasion and tax exemptions are indirectly documented.

Figure 2-17 also shows that, surprisingly, the ratio of final consumption to GDP has not fallen in Greece since 2010. This paradox demonstrates the importance of the aforementioned effect of internally devaluing predominately the private sector while that process in the public sector lagged behind. This suggests that the longstanding crowding-out effect of the public sector in Greece vis-à-vis the productive sector (see Malliaropoulos 2011) was not corrected during the first years of the conditionality program. It also suggests that the high impact of state spending on the excessive consumption observed in Greece also was not corrected, despite the steady decline in absolute income levels.

Having excluded indirect taxes as the main source of Greek revenue shortfall, the data reveal that the origin of the shortfall lies in direct taxes—and income taxes in particular. It should be further stressed that this discrepancy was not related to corporate income taxes, which for all European countries constitute a smaller share of total direct tax payments than do personal income taxes or other direct taxes. Rather, it was related to the low level of contributions from personal income taxes. The picture is completed by social security contributions made by salaried employees (as a percentage of GDP) that are only 2 percent lower than the European average (in spite of the much lower prevalence of dependent employment in Greece) and by the fact that the social security contributions of the numerous self-employed in Greece as a percentage of GDP are comparable with the average contribution of the self-employed segment in Europe.[7]

Thus we conclude that there were above-average social security contributions per employee in Greece for salaried employees and contributions below average for the self-employed. It should be noted that while the former case has not changed since 2010, the social security contributions of the self-employed have increased significantly as a result of changes in the laws since 2010.[8] But generally these still are flat contributions that do not vary with real income, and thus they constitute a proportionally larger burden on those self-employed with smaller incomes and a lighter burden on those with higher incomes.

The excessive progressivity of the tax burden in Greece up to 2012, which essentially exempted the vast majority of taxpayers from any meaningful income tax, has been identified by Mitsopoulos and Pelagidis (2012) as the main cause for the shortfall in tax revenue. This changed starting in 2012, with a significant reduction of the tax-free annual income threshold, from 12,000 down to only 5,000 euros a year. But at the same time, the anticipated benefit of this change is now offset by the decline in the tax base due to the aggressive internal devaluation of incomes of exactly those taxpayers that were the largest net contributors to general government revenue, that is, private sector employees with above-average salaries.

In addition, it is this group of taxpayers who are also most likely to be burdened by the new property taxes, now among the highest, if not the highest, in the OECD. In the past even the European Commission (EC 2012a) has not been able to distinguish between the taxes for which the legislation had been enacted and those that had not been collected or processed by the tax authorities for various reasons (for example, administrative inefficiency or the political calculation that the taxes should not be verified prior to elections). As a result, the tax authorities kept demanding ever higher property taxes in Greece even though the aggregate burden of the existing taxes had already reached levels unprecedented in any OECD country. A comparison of the budgeted recurrent property tax revenue (as a percentage of GDP) in Greece with the actual property tax revenue documented by the OECD (2012b) easily demonstrates this fact. Furthermore, the rapid increase in the number of households that owed property taxes, according to data from the Ministry of Economy in December 2013, clearly shows the increasing discrepancy between the ability of households to pay these taxes and the tax revenue expected by the authorities.[9] This observation is further supported by the very high taxes on property transactions, as documented by the OECD (2011b), a state of affairs exacerbated by the fact that administratively set prices often significantly exceeded the market prices. The latter, given the large increase in taxation, have factored in the future negative tax dividend and have understandably plummeted even while the administratively set prices have remained at the levels that predated the increase in these taxes. It should be added here that the recommendation of the OECD (2010) to shift the tax burden from labor and corporate activities to property and consumption follows from an analysis of local, rather than global, maximization and also does not account for a depressed economy with an acute liquidity crisis where property forms a disproportionally large portion of collateral and where the property market is burdened by significant institutional and policy failings.[10]

A careful reading of the data from the budgets of past years and of the 2013 budget of the Greek government shows how the ratio of net ordinary budget revenue (of the central government, including mainly tax revenue) to GDP has increased since the onset of the crisis. Interestingly, this relationship exists despite a fall in revenue because there has been an even steeper decline in GDP. Thus all the new taxes have largely succeeded in eliminating the deficit of tax revenue with respect to GDP that existed in Greece in the past. On the other hand, the primary expenditures of the central government, while decreasing, have fallen less than GDP, and thus this ratio has increased as well. General government data reveal, especially during the first years of the adjustment program, a much larger decline in total expenditure when compared to central government data. This reflects the fact that the consolidation of costs for some general government entities had been proceeding faster than at the central government level. In turn, this was due largely to cuts in pensions, which have reduced the expenditure of social security funds; to reduced prices for pharmaceuticals, which have decreased the related bill for medical insurance funds; and to improvements in key publicly owned enterprises (for example, fare increases for public transport and trains, elimination of unprofitable routes, and restructuring of rail operations).

Still, the noninterest expenditure of the general government, as a percentage of GDP, may have corrected from the excesses of 2009, but,

Figure 2-18. *Greek General Government Expenditure (Except Interest)*
and Revenue to GDP, 1988–2012

Percent of GDP

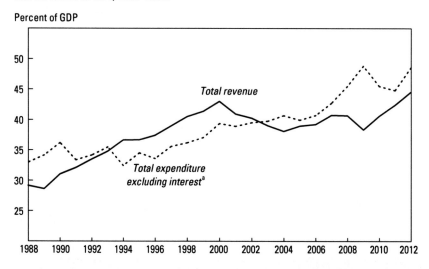

Source: European Commission, AMECO database, URTG, UUTGI (according to ESA, 2013 pending final confirma-
tion by Eurostat and thus excluded) (http://ec.europa.eu/economy_finance/ameco/user/serie/SelectSerie.cfm).
a. For 2012 costs that amount to 2.7 percent of GDP related to the recapitalization of MFIs are included.

especially given the rapid fall in GDP, a significant drop below the levels
before 2004 has not been observed so far (figure 2-18), even while total
revenue to GDP has increased significantly since 2009. These developments are in line with the findings of Mitsopoulos and Pelagidis (2012)
that the implementation of the adjustment program was predominantly
focused on revenue increases rather than cost cutting. In relation to this,
the claims often made with respect to the large decline in expenditure
since 2009 simply reflect the fact that expenditure increased exponentially
during the 2004–09 period, and especially in 2009, and was then partly
brought down from these very high levels. Therefore it remains a fact
that the decision to base the fiscal consolidation effort predominantly on
revenue increases exposes the process disproportionately to the risks associated with the rapid decline in the tax base. A final note should be made
regarding the large drop in interest payments, which is predominantly the
result of the ten-year derogation in interest payments offered to Greece by
the European Financial Stability Facility (EFSF).[11]

Even while the previous analysis suggests the scope for further expenditure cuts, to correctly evaluate the relatively large public sector wage
bill, one also has to compare public sector employment in Greece with

Figure 2-19. *Employment in Public Administration over Total Population, 2008–12*

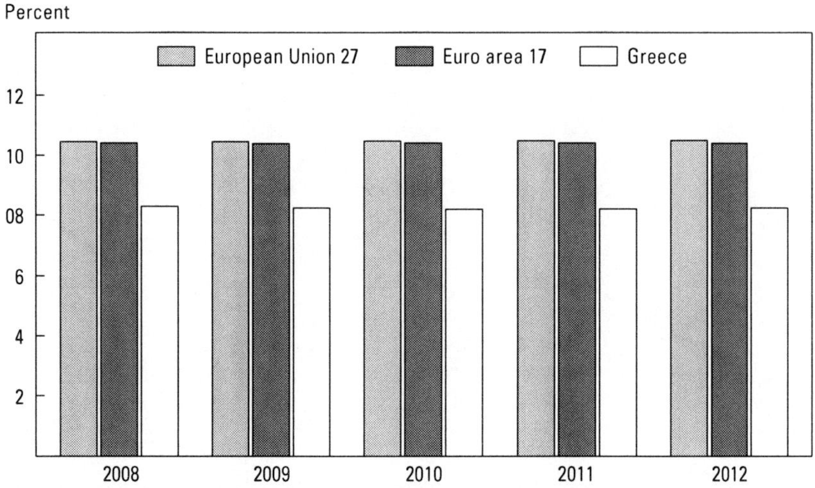

Percent

Source: Eurostat (http://epp.eurostat.ec.europa.eu/portal/page/portal/statistics/search_database).

that of other countries and with private sector employment, both within Greece and other countries. The number of Greek government employees (as estimated by employment in the NACE 2–designated sectors of public administration, defense, education, and health —including those employed in public schools, universities, and hospitals) does not seem to be excessive as a percentage of the total Greek population when compared with other euro area countries (figure 2-19). But it does seem excessive when compared to the number of private sector employees or with total employment (figure 2-20) elsewhere in the EU and euro area.

This observation is the consequence mainly of the low level of private sector employment rather than the high level of public sector employment. Thus the principal challenge in paying for the public sector wage bill is to increase private sector employment rather than decrease public sector employment. This assessment is even more applicable since the internal devaluation of the private sector during the past years has worsened this ratio. An additional factor that must be considered is the high per capita remuneration within the public sector when compared to the private sector average, as documented by the EC (2013c). In view of this situation, the main problem facing public sector human resource management is qualitative rather than quantitative. Employment reforms needed

Figure 2-20. *Employment in Public Administration, Defense, Health and Education over All Other Employment, 2008–12*

Percent

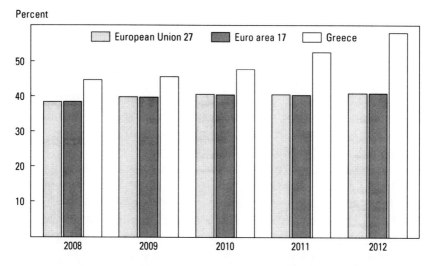

Source: Eurostat (http://epp.eurostat.ec.europa.eu/portal/page/portal/statistics/search_database).

extend beyond further rationalization of the pay structure in the public sector; they need to increase private sector employment, improve human resource management in the public sector, curtail massive and indiscriminate layoffs—and thereby constructively deal with the combination of fiscal challenges and the organizational problems of the public sector.

The Greek Financial System: A Difficult Adjustment and Some Core Policy Failures

The Greek government was asked to implement far-reaching and difficult changes to its fiscal structure. In complying, policymakers committed strategic errors such as imposing a disproportionately large internal devaluation on the private sector, the main tax base, while making much milder adjustments to government expenditures and the general public sector. For many years Greek political leadership had encouraged the development of a quasi-Soviet economy at the fringes of free markets. Now the political leadership and the administration ostensibly had agreed to tear down the bureaucracy they and their predecessors had established over the course of thirty years, while being offered the cash and support by the European Union and the IMF to keep operating largely in a "business as usual" way.

In particular, there was no apparent effort to rebalance policies to favor the private sector as a necessary precondition for success. After 2010 there were a number of unfortunate policy errors made by both the Greek government and its official lenders that further burdened the private sector even as they maintained the life-support systems for the profligate state. These policy errors included

—gradual acceptance of macroeconomic imbalances as permanent,

—the PSI, and particularly the large PSI of October 2011, as outlined in the respective euro area summit statements, and

—generation of uncertainty by tying the European prospects of the whole of Greece to the insufficient willingness of the government to implement the agreed-on program.

Overall, these questionable policies managed to subject the private sector of the economy to a full-blown liquidity crisis on top of the burdens of persistent fiscal problems, lack of nonwage cost competitiveness, and the inevitable adjustment taking place due to the fiscal retraction.

Exit from the Euro Area

The European partners responded on short notice to a request for financial assistance by the Greek government and offered a support package that stretched the spirit of the no-bailout clause—the first pillar of the Maastricht Treaty—to the limit.[12] For this they were rewarded, at best, with an unfortunate reluctance by successive Greek governments to face the grave problems at hand with adequate resolve. It was thus inevitable that at some point some European officials would mention the possibility of terminating, directly or indirectly, the membership of a misbehaving country, such as Greece. This meant, in turn, these officials were questioning the second pillar of the Maastricht Treaty, that once a country is in, it stays in.

The airing of such an option may have been a conscious or unconscious effort to force the habitually underresponsive Greek government to finally deal more decisively with its core problems. It may also reflect the reasonable doubts and disappointment of European politicians who are, it must be remembered, elected and accountable to the voters of their country. While the 1990–93 Greek government was aware that the rest of Europe also was going through a crisis at that time and that Greece had to take care of its own problems resolutely, such an awareness seems to be completely absent from the thinking of Greek politicians, at least during the first three years of the adjustment program. This indifference definitely undermined the efforts of European policymakers to help Greece within the limitations of the democratic mandates of the national and European governments, in spite of their often clearly demonstrated willingness to do so.

Yet opening a discussion about terminating Greece's membership in the euro area ultimately proved counterproductive. It can be argued that this possibility helped create a self-fulfilling prophecy, leading to conditions that favored Greece's exit from the euro area. Two elements have had an important impact on the trajectory of events: first, the increasing insistence that the Greek government achieve fiscal targets as a precondition for continuing its membership in the euro area, and second, the lack of legal provisions clarifying the links, if any, between an exit from the euro area and a complete exit from the European Union. The uncertainty these elements generated had a profound impact on Greece's economy. During 2012 one had only to approach the board of any international company to propose a project that involved investing in Greece and then watch the reaction or observe the flow of deposits out of Greek banks before early 2012 to appreciate how this uncertainty intensified the liquidity crisis and the depression of the Greek economy. Due to this uncertainty, the private sector already was effectively operating outside the euro area from early 2011. Increasingly, financing terms for Greek companies diverged from those in other euro area countries; trade credit, letters of credit, and export insurance no longer applied in Greece; and Greek companies doing business with parties from other euro areas were asked by their partners to pay cash for orders and prove the availability of matching cash deposited in accounts in other euro area countries. And as the official lenders imposed a debt-forgiveness program that burdened the private sector (by drastically reducing the value of Greek government bonds held by private investors) while reducing the interest payments on public sector debt to very low levels for the next decade, the availability and the cost of financing kept worsening for the private sector. This financial bottleneck led to a severe liquidity crisis and finally to a textbook-style, full-blown depression.[13] The Greek government was granted the backing of the EU partners in return for the promise to undertake necessary reforms; but once the Greek government got the EU assurance, it failed to faithfully deliver on that promise. The subsequent strategy of tying the European future of Greece to the actions of its government was based on the assumption that the Greek government actually represents the Greek people and acts in their best interest, honoring their democratic mandate. However, given the decades of clientelistic policies, kleptocracy, and manipulation of benefits to favor the state and special interest groups that thrive on state-sponsored privileges—while all the costs, burdens, and restrictions have been placed upon the private sector—one could have easily questioned this assumption.

Such questions are also justified by the fact that corruption in Greece has had an important impact on the trajectory of the political system in the decades preceding the current crisis. As corrupt officials and politicians allegedly pocketed hundreds of millions of euros from foreign companies that had won lucrative state procurement contracts in Greece, the noncorrupt politicians and officials were outgunned in the political arena. They simply could not match the clout of their opponents who had almost unlimited resources to buy media coverage, court political allies, and form allegiances cemented by corrupt procurement deals.

According to domestic and international investigations, court rulings, and pleas, there were numerous corruption cases involving Greek ministers and political figures where international companies had paid large bribes to Greek officials. (German companies were prominently involved; see appendix A.) Such financial support of corrupt politicians and administrations by foreign corporations—not just the Greek private sector— may have significantly affected the trajectory of domestic politics. Thus many Greeks believed that they were being unjustly punished by those who financially supported corrupt politicians yet were asking the people to bear all the costs of the failings of their political representatives. Greek voters were likely to express their frustration with this at the polls, generating increased political uncertainty, a risk that further inhibited the flow of funds into the country, effectively increasing the financial isolation of the productive parts of the Greek economy.[14]

Therefore the demands on successive Greek governments to do what was necessary were morally right but neither constructive nor effective. A different approach would have been not to call Greece's European prospects into question but rather to call into question the nonvital parts of the funding of a government that had failed to deliver on its part of the unprecedented deal. While such an approach would have required innovative political thinking and institutional maneuvering, if elegantly executed it would have ultimately avoided the moral hazards that are so evident in the politically orthodox strategy adopted.

Furthermore, the strategy adopted by the official lenders of the Greek government has undermined—albeit unintentionally—the efforts of those

Greek groups who desire reform and want Greece to completely pay its debts. Instead, the adopted strategy has effectively supported, and still supports, those in the country who use the increasing desperation of the population as a weapon to stave off meaningful reforms. The uncertainty resulting from linking Greece's European prospects to the performance of its government has directly influenced public opinion as to who is expected to prevail in Greece's internal struggle. In this context supporters of reform have to deal with a major impediment: it is difficult for those challenging the status quo to gain widespread support when their opponents appear to have, effectively, major international financial backing. Unfortunately, the fall of the reform-minded government in 1993 reinforces the belief that supporting reformers ultimately means supporting the losers—a choice that is by definition unpopular and that under most circumstances would be irrational. It also should be noted here that those who championed effective and honest reforms within the administration, even during the past three years, have not only *not* been rewarded but also have been confronted by immense personal costs and, in some cases, a certain end to their political careers.

Another manifestation of flawed policy concerns the manner in which the conditionality program has been implemented, as it may lead to a repeat of the economic disaster of the 1980s. At that time Greek companies faced international competition as a result of accession to the European market while domestically they encountered an increasingly hostile regulatory and business environment. In the current situation, Greek policymakers and the official lenders seem to place market deregulation for tradables ahead of the improvement of the business environment, and therefore Greek companies—still facing the burdens of an adverse business environment, red tape, overregulated network industries, increased energy prices, and, now, a full-blown liquidity crisis—will stand no chance in an environment where only the "obstacles to market entry" are selectively removed. While removal of the latter is a precondition for Greece to be able to reap the benefits of free markets, failure to address the rest of the burdens on the private sector will lead to the complete decimation of the remaining productive base of the country and thus eliminate any hope of long-term, sustainable high growth rates and satisfactory employment levels (Mitsopoulos 2014).

Since the private sector already effectively operates outside the euro area, the ramifications of a potential exit from the euro area—and thereby possibly from the European Union itself—may extend well beyond economic impacts to the reality that it would mean the final loss of the only remaining forces preventing a complete submission of all Greek institutions to the corrupt forces of the past decades. Thus an exit from the euro area would mean that Greece would become one of the most failed countries on the planet. A European policy to encourage such an exit thus amounts to condemning Greek—*European*—citizens to the collective punishment of being relegated to life in a failed state. The belief that Greece could better implement the necessary reforms outside the euro area demonstrates a seriously inadequate understanding of the political and social dynamics at work in the country. It indicates a failure to take into account the "political economy of reform," an issue that only the OECD, among the major international organizations, has recently started to investigate in greater detail (OECD 2009).

A strategy to restore the certainty of Greece's European prospects and force those responsible for the current situation to face the consequences of their actions could involve options such as removing control of legislative initiatives from the government if they are not sufficiently growth-enhancing (see Trichet 2012). This would inevitably be part of a credible threat to a compromised government and in line with a deepening of the policy coordination in the EU. However, such an approach must be limited only to growth-enhancing measures and must refrain from strategies linked to further tax increases and socially unjust initiatives, as the latter would very rapidly—and justifiably—turn public opinion against such legislation, in spite of the Greek government. In that sense an automatic implementation of EU legislation, which the Greek government has failed to properly do, would be within the bounds of the democratic mandate of the European legislators and the guarantor of treaties.

Finally, questioning the "once in, always in" principle (possibly as a response to the incautious questioning of the "no-bailout clause" by the Greek government in the spring of 2010) has wide-ranging implications not only for Greece but also for the future of the common currency, as it undermines confidence in the common currency area. The belief that tight supervision of public finances will ensure that Greece's current problems will not be faced by any other euro area country is based on the assumption that James Madison's angels, described in *Federalist Paper 51,* will always govern all member states.[15] But unless the markets are confident that all member states will stay in the union, the currency risk will be present even if the currency at issue is the euro. The Canadian dollar was used as a currency in Quebec even as the uncertainty of secession caused companies to migrate from Montreal to Toronto, and the euro is the currency of Greece even while a euro in a Greek bank or offered by a Greek company is not treated the same way as a euro in a German bank or offered by a German company. To dispel the fears of the markets that any member state could be expelled, in direct or indirect ways, European leaders have to support the idea of a united Europe with more determination, extending their commitment beyond the current plans for a closer fiscal supervision (see EC 2011a) and a "banking union." The forging of a lasting union, "so conceived and so dedicated that can long endure," as the creation of another, differently structured union over 200 years ago demonstrated, is not accomplished upon completion of the work of the inspired and determined "founding fathers." It is an ongoing process that depends on the determination demonstrated every day to face challenges that threaten the integrity of the union.

The developments in Cyprus since the spring of 2013 exemplify the risks associated with Greece's uncertain European prospects since the markets still doubt that country's ability to meet its fiscal targets on the basis of a drastically "internally devalued" tax base and the predictability of the domestic political developments. The terms for recapitalization of Greek banks do not go toward aggressively stabilizing a severely depressed economy. The same is true regarding the political ploy of replacing "Grexit talk" at the European level with statements and acts suggesting that already nervous Greek depositors are not absolutely secure against a bail-in. As Greece still depends predominantly on traditional banking to finance its business economy, quickly improving access to sound financing for the private sector is only possible if substantial amounts of money—on a scale commensurate with the current dependence of the domestic financial system on the Eurosystem—start flowing into the country's banks from depositors and investors. However, significant input from the latter group will occur only if confidence is supported and allowed to return.

The Liquidity Squeeze of a Depressed Economy

Deposits in domestic financial institutions, by households, businesses and the general government, declined by about 100 billion euros between December 2009 and the summer of 2012, as shown in figure 2-21. This outflow can be linked to uncertainties with regard to the possible bankruptcy of the state, exit from the euro area, rumors that undeclared moneys would be ferreted out, taxation of deposits, and the need of

Figure 2-21. *Deposits, Greek MFIs, Except Covered Bonds, 2001–13*[a]

Billions of euros

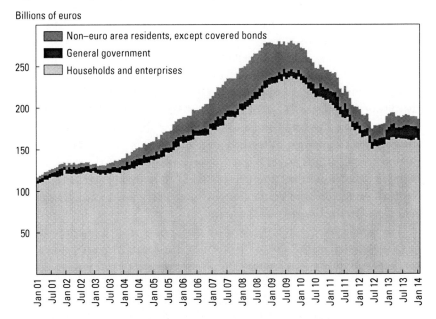

Source: Bank of Greece (www.bankofgreece.gr/Pages/el/Statistics/monetary/deposits.aspx).
a. MFI, main financial institutions.

households and businesses to cover current tax payments and expenses that can no longer be financed by their cash flow. In early 2012 this was also exacerbated by political uncertainty following repeated elections; however, the ultimate formation of a coalition government led to the stabilization of the deposits starting in early summer 2012. The gradual increase in deposits since then reflected a return of the confidence in the safety of the Greek banking system, but during 2013 this trend halted as talk of a bail-in replaced that of a euro-exit and as the unreasonably high property taxes forced households to tap increasingly into their savings in order to pay them during late 2013.

During this same period, financing of the private sector and the general government initially proved relatively resilient despite the emerging financing gap, but at the same time, new access to liquidity essentially dried up (see ECB 2012). Financing of the general government declined in the summer of 2011, following the write-down of the first PSI (PSI1, decided in July 2011; European Council 2011a), and again in 2012 after

Figure 2-22. *Replenishing of the Financing Gap of Greek MFIs—
Access to Eurosystem, 2001–13*

Billions of euros

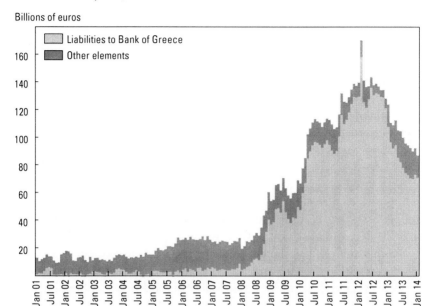

Source: Bank of Greece.

the second, larger PSI (PSI2, decided in October 2011; European Council 2011b); neither decrease reflected a repayment of loans but rather the losses incurred by the holders of these bonds, that is, primarily Greek main financial institutions and social security funds. Furthermore, this decline in general government financing is observed only after a significant increase in this financing, as Greek banks acquired large amounts of Greek government bonds ahead of the government's request for official assistance in early 2010. Foreign banks that had significant holdings of such bonds had unloaded most of them on European central banks ahead of the PSI.

This financing gap, resulting from the simultaneous outflow of deposits and the resilience of the financing provided to the private sector and the general government, was filled through access to the Eurosystem, as shown in figure 2-22. This access and emergency liquidity assistance (ELA; more expensive but more flexible with respect to collateral at some points during late 2011 and early 2012) allowed the Greek financial system to deal with the massive outflow of deposits.[16] The Hellenic Financial Stability Fund's replenishment part of the losses incurred by Greek banks from PSI1 and especially PSI2 may have restored supervisory capital to levels that allowed the systemic Greek banks ("too large to fail") to participate in the Eurosystem; but in the end these sums were marginal compared with the outflow of deposits.

As figure 2-22 shows, the commitment of the Eurosystem to the Greek financial system exceeded 160 billion euros by early 2012, covering essentially about one-third of the balance sheet total, even though the intricacies suggested by Soros (2012) must be taken into account here. While the Greek financial system's dependence on the Eurosystem—especially the ELA—has been reduced during 2013, it remains at a high level, and a further reduction of this dependence, as planned for 2015 and 2017, will pose a challenge for the availability of liquidity to the private sector, unless Greek banks regain sufficient access to wholesale market financing and the deposit base recovers strongly.

As this analysis has shown, restoring the trust of markets in Greece's prospects within the euro area is the key to ensuring that the liability side of Greek financial institutions is no longer dependent on the liquidity provided by the Eurosystem. It also has illustrated that market trust is much more important for ensuring the financing of the Greek economy and overcoming the financing challenges faced by Greek companies (OECD 2012a) than was restoring the core supervisory capital after the blow to the Greek banks from the PSI2 of October 2011, even if that step was obviously a prerequisite. Other initiatives, such as financing provided by European programs and the European Investment Bank (EIB) certainly can help.[17] However, as the size of the financing gap replenished by the Eurosystem demonstrates, the effect of such initiatives will be marginal as long as the aggregate financing of the Greek financial system is subject to a significant national and political risk. If some normality is to return to the Greek economy, then the Greek government must implement initiatives that comply with the conditionality program—especially the structural reforms—and the European leadership needs to implement policies that ensure Greece's European prospects and secure the viability of the financial system and the security of Greek deposits proportionately to the extraordinary nature of the circumstances at hand.[18] Furthermore, all the foregoing actions must be boldly adapted to the reality of the extraordinary circumstances of a full-blown depression and liquidity crisis. As of this writing, only the ECB has demonstrated, with the extensive and flexible terms it has offered to Greek banks, that it broadly understands the nature of the ongoing liquidity crisis. And yet the unprecedented easing adopted by the ECB during the past years has failed to improve the financing conditions for companies in countries like Greece, in spite of the unprecedented efforts of Greek banks to strengthen their balance sheets and in spite of the fact that by now they have the most transparent balance sheets in Europe, thus demonstrating the fragmented state of the financial services market as well as of the monetary policy transmission mechanism in the euro area.

At this stage the prolonged depression of the Greek economy has additional implications that must be taken into account. The recession had significantly eroded the Greek GDP as early as 2011, thus increasing the debt of the private sector in Greece as a percentage of GDP to a level above the euro area average (figure 2-23). Of course, the government debt has long been and remains excessive as a percentage of GDP, in spite of the PSI, given the continual and rapid shrinking of the GDP.

Now the Greek depression is gradually degrading the quality of the loan portfolios and the value of collateral, meaning that in addition to the short-term pressures on the system, the medium-term dynamics are going to pose new challenges. Furthermore, businesses and households are facing a financing cost that may not appear dramatic in absolute terms but constitutes a very heavy burden once the cost of money is compared to the evolution of nominal GDP and when compared to the very low cost of money for other European businesses, as shown in figure 2-24. In addition, when the scarcity of available financing is taken into account, these developments form a process that not only erodes the balance sheets of banks, companies, and households but also increasingly generates profoundly adverse effects on the daily life and society of the country—a Greek "Great Depression." Such exceptional circumstances rationally call for exceptional support measures going well beyond the terms and conditions that form the basis of the current vision for a "banking union." These baseline terms and conditions may be insufficient to deal with such extreme circumstances in an isolated part of the (now fragmented) common currency and single supervisory area, and may require unorthodox approaches, in the spirit of Hamilton (1790) and like the ones proposed, for example, by Kirkegaard (2014).[19]

In closing, we want to stress that the current financing conditions faced by Greek companies are simply not sustainable in the long term; if prolonged, they will lead to the complete devastation of the Greek corporate landscape. In addition, the protracted full-blown liquidity crisis for the private sector and the persistent depression of the economy as a whole,

Figure 2-23. *Private Sector and General Government Debt, 2011*

Percent of GDP

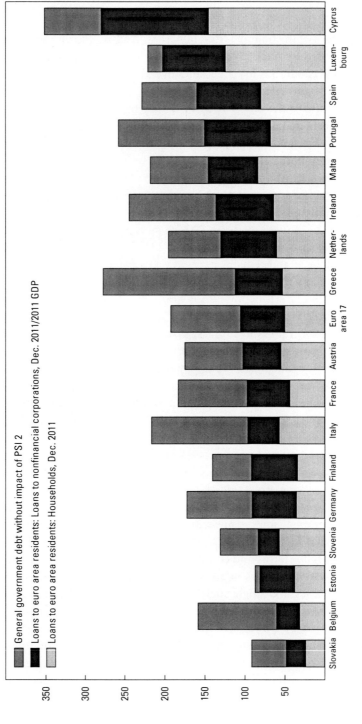

Source: ECB, "MFI Balance Sheets, Euro Area, 2.2 Loans" (http://sdw.ecb.europa.eu/home.do); Eurostat (http://epp.eurostat.ec.europa.eu/portal/page/portal/statistics/search_database).

Figure 2-24. *Cost of Financing to Nonfinancial Companies, Deviation from Euro Area Average, 2008–14*[a]

Percentage points

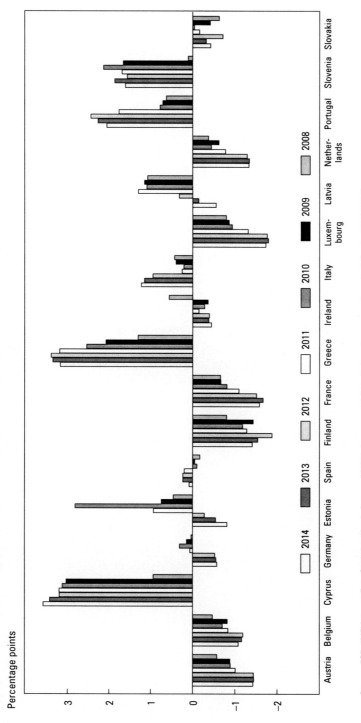

Source: ECB, "MFI Interest Rate Statistics. Yearly Average" (2014, January only) (http://sdw.ecb.europa.eu/reports.do?node=1000003503)

a. Credit and other institutions (MFI except MMFs and central banks). Loans up to 1 year, annualized agreed rate (AAR)/narrowly defined effective rate (NDER). Total, nonfinancial corporations (S.11). Difference between euro area average and national yearly average.

along with new challenges like the increased cost of energy, have eroded to dangerous levels the balance sheets of many companies that otherwise would have viable business models in spite of the challenges posed by the business environment in Greece. The absence of an adequate infrastructure, that is, available operational units and know-how, to manage especially those companies that can rebound and contribute to the recovery of the economy, in addition to the deficiencies of the institutional framework (for example, bankruptcy law and related proceedings, an adequate framework to encourage direct investment in companies that do not have the size to gain access to the corporate bond market, and the securitization of such investments) may still prove fatal to a significant part of the productive sector of the country. Dealing with these shortcomings and initiating policies to directly address the liquidity crisis are not only prerequisites for restoring employment and economic activity but are central to assisting the resolute recovery of the Greek economy; they should occur in tandem with actions to achieve the fiscal targets set by the official lenders and the European Semester.[20] In a sense, addressing these issues will also contribute toward encouraging nonbank financing in the Greek economy, a trend that has to be actively supported at the European level as well if the current European policy stance to deleverage financial intermediation is not to form a long-term drag on the growth prospects of the Union.

3

Unlocking Growth
Innovation as a Driver of
Competitiveness and Prosperity

In most statistical surveys Greece appears to perform poorly in innovation, R&D, and related activities. The European Commission Innovation Scoreboard and the INSEAD Global Innovation Index are only two of the many publications that essentially identify Greece as a below-average innovator. Most of these studies agree on the weaknesses of the country's innovation system. All of them also identify the challenges related especially to private sector funding, linkages between entrepreneurship and researchers, and the accumulation of intellectual assets. The latter two also figure in the Eurostat data demonstrating how before the crisis (2007–08) the bulk of the shortage of in-house R&D spending could be attributed to the business community rather than to the Greek higher education system, which is solely financed under the Greek constitution via government funding, and direct government funding (see figure 3-1).

The business community's weak R&D spending is positively correlated with numerous other performance indicators, such as the low employment of scientists and low patent activity (OECD 2011c). And the Innovation Union Scoreboard (EC 2011b, 2013b) finds that Greece has below-average levels of medium- and high-tech product exports, as a percentage of all product exports, and that it has a low percentage of knowledge-intensive service exports compared with total service exports. This lackluster showing is compatible with other observations that reflect aspects of the structure of the whole economy. The World Bank's Worldwide Governance Indicators (WGI) and the World Economic Forum's (WEF) Global Competitiveness Report (GCR) also rank Greece clearly below the majority of developed nations, as shown in table 3-1.

Figure 3-1. *Business Enterprise, Government, and Tertiary Institution Spending on R&D as Percentage of GDP, 2007*[a]

Percent (total intramural R&D expenditures [GERD] by sectors of performance)

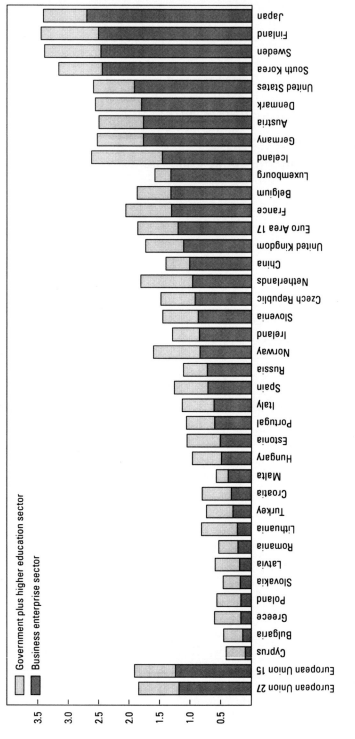

Legend:
- Government plus higher education sector
- Business enterprise sector

Source: Eurostat.
a. Country notes: China does not include Hong Kong.

Table 3-1. Ranking of Greece versus Other Countries on Innovation and Governance Indexes, 2011[a]

Index ranking

Rank among 125 countries of sample	Greece	Australia	Austria	Belgium	Finland	France	Germany	Ireland	Israel	Japan	Portugal	Spain	Sweden	Argentina	Armenia	Bahrain	Botswana	Brazil	Bulgaria	China	India	Indonesia	Italy	Peru	Romania	Turkey	Uruguay	Burkina Faso	Burundi	Cambodia	Cameroon	Honduras	Kenya	Nicaragua	Venezuela	Zambia	Zimbabwe	Albania	Vietnam
Company spending on R&D, 1–7 (best)	119	27	17	19	4	15	5	21	8	1	41	46	2	69	109	94	71	30	93	23	33	31	34	110	83	61	55	97	121	63	52	79	29	114	112	54	106	50	51
Property rights, 1–7 (best)	52	23	12	27	1	11	18	10	31	20	46	43	5	118	84	19	36	54	105	40	62	75	64	80	76	65	39	63	119	83	92	86	91	107	125	66	124	103	87
Intellectual property protection, 1–7 (best)	50	19	16	26	1	7	13	10	34	22	41	42	4	116	88	20	48	77	92	46	64	58	55	110	90	100	47	80	124	83	89	71	91	107	125	60	82	86	115
Burden of government regulation, 1–7 (best)	117	69	44	112	10	103	80	54	61	67	113	97	25	115	47	4	26	125	78	20	87	39	124	106	94	84	74	42	60	31	82	49	83	65	122	27	73	8	100
Quality of overall infrastructure, 1–7 (best)	59	37	8	17	6	3	10	50	38	13	12	22	11	97	71	19	54	94	111	65	79	75	72	95	124	34	62	117	119	70	109	82	74	105	114	86	103	67	110
Quality of the educational system, 1–7 (best)	107	12	23	6	3	32	16	11	44	34	69	89	8	78	88	29	53	102	92	49	36	41	80	114	82	86	75	111	123	62	71	115	26	120	108	48	31	42	63
Intensity of local competition, 1–7 (best)	75	7	8	2	65	12	9	56	27	4	53	23	10	94	123	25	69	45	91	22	30	81	55	52	89	13	93	115	100	80	82	90	62	105	124	68	86	108	59
Burden of customs procedures, 1–7 (best)	75	19	20	41	3	30	36	16	32	35	34	42	4	124	118	8	33	112	101	54	85	81	76	51	110	89	61	73	117	86	74	78	109	114	125	65	84	63	103
Flexibility of wage determination, 1–7 (best)	118	101	123	113	116	46	119	107	37	14	96	112	120	122	35	4	81	100	52	41	47	98	117	22	78	43	125	54	11	74	75	90	70	80	111	73	124	61	18
Venture capital availability, 1–7 (best)	98	21	40	20	9	35	36	100	2	44	68	56	6	118	102	8	43	49	62	22	27	17	93	37	72	77	70	124	125	57	109	75	28	104	105	108	120	115	86
Domestic market size index, 1–7 (best)	33	17	35	28	52	8	5	36	50	4	43	13	32	21	102	108	90	8	63	2	3	16	10	42	41	15	79	101	124	88	81	98	70	100	34	106	122	91	37
Value chain breadth, 1–7 (best)	81	73	5	16	7	8	4	15	13	1	42	24	2	86	109	46	108	50	82	43	40	28	11	87	98	47	68	123	122	76	85	58	45	100	125	102	124	118	96
Quality of scientific research institutions, 1–7 (best)	84	13	21	5	18	15	10	16	1	11	23	39	4	41	101	96	76	42	74	38	34	53	55	103	85	83	56	63	116	82	89	105	51	118	106	67	99	121	70
Control of corruption: Estimate	60	8	22	16	4	20	15	19	35	21	25	27	3	78	95	45	29	49	61	94	86	96	57	64	63	50	23	75	118	117	110	106	109	102	123	83	125	91	89
Government effectiveness: Estimate	48	10	14	13	1	22	17	20	26	23	34	30	4	77	71	43	47	67	65	59	68	81	49	76	80	51	44	92	120	106	116	98	94	117	121	103	122	78	83
Regulatory quality: Estimate	48	8	17	22	9	26	15	11	20	35	42	27	6	112	66	38	49	69	46	84	94	91	39	50	40	55	57	81	119	103	115	79	82	96	124	101	125	65	108
Rule of law: Estimate	45	9	7	20	1	19	16	10	33	23	30	24	2	92	77	51	42	60	64	79	63	95	50	93	58	56	41	75	118	114	116	110	113	96	124	83	125	86	82
Voice and accountability: Estimate	37	10	12	13	6	18	15	16	42	29	21	23	4	54	98	115	50	45	48	124	53	71	33	64	52	78	22	87	110	104	113	91	83	96	105	81	122	62	123

Sources: World Economic Forum, "Global Competitiveness Report, 2011–2012" (www.weforum.org/reports/global-competitiveness-report-2011-2012); World Bank, "Worldwide Governance Indicators," 2011 (http://info.worldbank.org/governance/wgi/index.aspx#home).

a. WEF GCI and World Bank Governance indicators. Some index variables may since have been affected by significant reforms, such as wage flexibility in Greece.

Stobbe and Pawlicki (2012) offer the perspective of a more comprehensive approach, singling out from among the weaknesses of the Greek innovation system the heavy dependence on imported technologies. In addition to the low share of business expenditure on R&D, they note the concentration thereof on a limited number of sectors such as IT services, consumer electronics, and pharmaceuticals. They further stress the domestic restrictions on financing innovation and start-up companies and note the weak uptake of available EU funds for innovation. Also, according to their analysis, Greece has only a small percentage of companies that can be classified as suppliers of high-technology or knowledge-intensive services. Finally, the authors point out the importance of shipping and stress the low diversification of service exports as a result of the predominance of tourism.

Yet there are also areas where Greece's performance in innovation is at least average or even above average. It is these comparatively strong areas that both make the persistent lag in business R&D expenditure so puzzling and suggest that some components may already be in place and could be built upon to help reverse the current undesirable situation. Thus the Innovation Union Scoreboard (EC 2011b, 2013b) finds that Greece has relative strength in human resources—albeit showing no increase in the 2013 scoreboard, indicating the impact of the brain drain resulting from the depression—and performs strongly on a number of indicators such as "the introduction of new innovations in the product lines of firms." The country also scores high in international scientific copublications and makes a decent showing for participation in highly cited publications, although performance in the realm of public-private scientific copublications is well below average (but not negligible). Greece scores above average in business spending on non-R&D innovation and about average for SMEs that innovate in-house and for inter-SME collaboration on innovation. Other findings include strong performance by SMEs in the introduction of marketing and organizational innovations and below average, but nonnegligible, employment in knowledge-intensive activities.

Stobbe and Pawlicki (2012) also record the relative strength in scientific activity as documented by the level of publications, although they do point out structural weaknesses in the data that evaluate the comprehensive performance of the educational system. They identify comparative advantages in certain sectors, such as fisheries, tobacco production, agriculture, food production, textiles, metal processing, printing, and the manufacture of rubber and plastics, chemicals, and pharmaceuticals. The pharmaceutical industry is identified as the only one in the medium-high technology segment, with the others classified in lower-tech categories. Additionally, INSEAD rankings (Cornell, INSEAD and WIPO 2013), using the WEF GCR subindexes, identify the development of and access to ICT and publication of scientific articles as areas of relative strength in Greece's innovation structure. In other dimensions of innovation, Greece lags other developed economies but still demonstrates that some non-negligible capacity exists, as in the quality of the (government-financed) research institutions and the development of clusters. But on some parameters—such as venture capital deals, gross expenditure on R&D, and computer and communications service exports—Greece's relative contribution is almost nonexistent (figure 3-2).

The demonstrated weaknesses and the existence of certain areas of strength, especially with respect to the quality of available research capacity, raise the question of the appropriate strategy to optimize existing strengths and ameliorate the weaknesses. Available evidence suggests that there is a noteworthy government-funded research capacity that could be employed for productive collaboration with a business community that has largely abstained from R&D-based innovation. While the Innovation Scoreboard provides evidence that Greek companies do innovate in certain areas, such as their product lines, the fact remains that the broader ability to innovate and to offer high value added products and services increasingly requires the input of research (see Wunsch-Vincent 2012; OECD 2011c), and that the link between the research centers and the business economy is, at best, very weak.

In light of recent developments, one must ask whether the severe economic crisis has changed Greece's innovation performance since 2008, and what prospects this crisis leaves for the country to be again internationally competitive through the use of domestic strengths in innovation. Regarding the first question, the 2008 Innovation Scoreboard (EC 2008) ranked Greece eighteenth back in 2007. Five years later it ranks nineteenth (EC 2011b). In both instances Greece falls in the moderate innovator category, toward the lower end of the innovation scale.

However low the Greek innovation performance might be, the average annual growth in innovation performance, at more than 4 percent, was remarkable before the crisis. This suggests, somewhat surprisingly, the significant potential for Greece to use innovation as a driver for competitiveness.

Using the Innovation Union Scoreboard terminology, innovation "leaders" in the EU-27, such as Sweden, Germany, Denmark, and Finland,

Figure 3-2. *Strengths and Weaknesses of the Greek Innovation Infrastructure versus Ireland, Portugal, United States, Germany, and Finland 2012*[a]

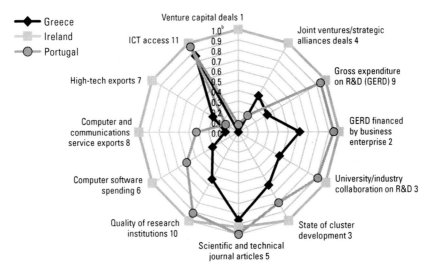

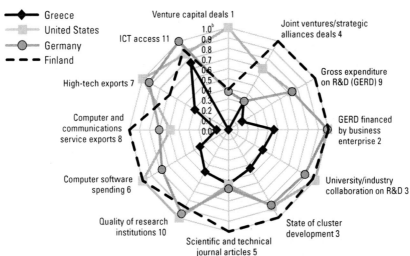

Source: Authors' calculations based on data from INSEAD Global Innovation Index (Cornell, INSEAD, and WIPO 2013).

a. Units of measure per indicator: 1—per trillion of GDP (Thomson One Banker Private Equity Database); 2—percent of total GERD (UNESCO); 3—index: min. 1, max. 7 (WEF); 4—per trillion dollars GDP (Thomson One Banker Private Equity Database); 5—articles per billion dollars GDP (National Science Foundation); 6—percent of GDP (World Bank World Development Indicators); 7—percent of exports, excluding re-exports (UN); 8—percent of commercial services exports; 9—percent of GDP; 10—questionnaire answer (WEF); 11—composite index (International Telecommunications Union).

b. Normalized, 1 is best of sample, 0 worst. GERD: gross expenditure on R&D.

continued to improve their performance, and some "followers" such as the United Kingdom, Luxemburg, the Netherlands, and France, approached their levels. However, some countries that lagged in innovation performance—the "modest" and "moderate" innovators—lost their momentum and fell further behind. Greece, with a 6 percent decline in innovation score from 2010 to 2012, was prominent among this struggling group of countries.

For countries such as Greece that had below-average innovation performance, their relative weaknesses are the paucity of finance performance and support, firm investments, economic effects, and intellectual assets. With respect to positive trends, under intellectual assets the registration of community designs is growing fast in Greece, and the level of internal scientific copublication has been quite high. On the other hand, venture capital investment has dropped and knowledge-intensive services exports have declined even more steeply.

The existing studies that attempt to map out the next steps for the Greek economy are often confined to an essentially linear extrapolation of precrisis success stories into the future. The official lenders' emphasis on the performance of tourism exemplifies such an approach. But even studies that also identify many strong sectors or sectors with much potential (see, for example, McKinsey 2012a; Stobbe and Pawlicki 2012) essentially extrapolate from past successes of the country into the future. It is perhaps only reasonable that they do not engage in the riskier exercise of envisioning the new, unanticipated, and undemonstrated combinations of economic activities that could grow out of existing ones and thus do not present a broader strategy for how the Greek economy could climb up the value chain from its starting point. Such an alternative approach would be more in line with the work of Rodrik, Hausmann, and Hwang (2006), who point out the need for a larger range of activities that can interact and in turn encourage innovation.

The analysis and recommendations in this chapter are based on this premise, that the existing sources of innovation and economic activity in Greece can be viewed as parts of a network complex enough to serve as a springboard for new activities and new combinations of activities.[1] To realize this potential, one must identify the prerequisite complimentary activities as well as those factors that currently impede them, thus alerting policymakers to their existence and enabling them to shape policies to help promising activities emerge. This wider focus by no means implies that Greece should not try to expand on the successes of the past or use its obvious comparative advantages in sectors such as tourism and

---

Box 3-1. *List of Major Greek Science and Business Parks*[a]

Patrai Science Park / University of Patras

Centre for Research and Technology Hellas in Thessaloniki (EKETA)

Thessaloniki ICT Business Park

Foundation for Research and Technology in Crete (ITE)

Corallia clusters initiative (ATHENS)

Scientific and Technological Park of Hepirous / University of Ioannina

Centre for Research and Technology—Thessaly National Centre for Scientific
Research (NCSR) / Technology Park of Thessaly

"Demokritos" and Technology and Science Park of Attika "Lefkippos"

Lavrion Technological and Cultural Park, National Technical University

Source: Pelagidis (2008).
a. More detailed information for each of them is available in the book of the first "Research and Innovation Prize" co-organized by SEV Hellenic Federation of Enterprises and Eurobank, 2010–11 (www.kainotomeis.gr). A presentation of major research universities is included in the book of the 2012–13 second competition (www.kainotomeis.gr). On the structure and organization of science and technology parks in Greece, see also Pelagidis (2008).

---

agriculture. Rather, it implies that there is also value in pursuing less obvious possibilities, which by definition will be more innovative.

Following this line of thought, we focus in this chapter on an area not covered by the foregoing studies, which either extrapolate from the past, are limited by analyzing the data from exporting sectors only, or only indirectly make note of this resource (for example, Stobbe and Pawlicki 2012): the stock of tangible and intangible assets existing in centers of excellence in universities and in science and business parks. Some of the main parks are listed in box 3-1, and all are associated with government-operated universities or research centers.

Most of these centers were set up with lavish public funding, yet were effectively, in some cases explicitly, prohibited by the existing institutional framework and the prevailing practices from collaborating with the business sector. Their above-average propensity to excel with respect to EU-funded programs is viewed as a success, but this can also be read as another manifestation of the fact that the avenues for accepting projects that originate from the domestic business community are significantly restricted.

In the subsequent analysis, we argue that the low level of business R&D and the low level of collaboration between businesses and research centers do not result from the unwillingness of Greek companies to be innovative and to finance research, as often wrongly argued by political leaders. Rather, we seek evidence for the proposition that the current poor performance of business R&D expenditures is a consequence of the insurmountable hurdles set up by the institutional framework that have made collaboration between the business community and the basically state-sponsored research community almost impossible. In the end we argue that the words of Senator Birch Bayh, quoted by Gulbranson and Audretsch (2008), could not have been more appropriate for Greece: "What sense does it make to spend billions of dollars each year on government-supported research and then prevent new developments from benefiting the American people because of dumb bureaucratic red tape?"

In the following section, we summarize the main observations and results of the largely recent literature that is relevant to these issues. In the process we identify aspects and possible factors that may affect the tendency of the business community to innovate and in particular to engage in R&D expenditure. We then analyze and interpret data that can specify and demonstrate the effects of these aspects, and then establish that the nature of institutional characteristics of a country can explain the low level of business R&D. In the third section we use the insights gained from the review of the literature and the data analysis to formulate proposals for policy initiatives that could help Greece make the most out of its existing advantages and infrastructure.

Drivers of Innovation and Their Status in Greece

To find explanations for the low level of business R&D expenditure in Greece, we reviewed the literature to identify key factors that are important for the encouragement of innovation, especially research-based innovation. The identification of these factors then made it possible to match the findings of the literature with the insights gained from five years of interviews with members of the business and research community in Greece.[2]

Role of Competitive Forces in Driving Innovation

Hard evidence (see, for example, Arnold, Nicoletti, and Scarpetta 2008) increasingly supports the thesis that competition, both downstream and upstream, is a necessary precondition for stimulating innovation through the adoption of new production processes and the evolution of the production input mix. For example, Nicodème and Sauner-Leroy (2004) stress the role of competitive markets in putting pressure on rents and creating incentives for companies both to reallocate (allocative efficiency) and use (productive efficiency) their resources in the most efficient way and, controlling for other variables, generally force competitors to innovate. Griffith, Harrison, and Simpson (2006) also find that product market reforms, and in particular the Single Market Program, had statistically and economically significant effects on the extent of competition, changes in innovative activity, and total factor productivity growth, even though they are unlikely to have been the most important factor in the Single European Market. They also suggest that a range of other factors are likely to have affected innovative activity and productivity growth over the period examined, such as human capital, infrastructure (broadly defined), and a range of other institutional elements.

Furthermore, innovative content often is larger in the organizational structure, which in turn often is harder to copy, than in the case of new technologies—despite the fact that new technologies often make the former possible in the first place—and this leads to significant differences in the various types of innovation. Incentives to innovate in processes and organizational forms, which in turn encourage solutions that can support such innovations, are generated by competitive forces in downstream markets; however, it is often competition and a level playing field, low administrative barriers, and low burdens to doing business in upstream markets that make adaptation of innovative production processes possible. The practical relevance of such an assertion is supported, for example, by the findings of Balasubramanian and Sivadasan (2011). They find that patent activity is associated with firm growth through new product innovations (firm scope) rather than through reduction in the cost of producing existing products (firm productivity), which in turn may depend on harder to copy organizational innovations. They also argue that these firms have a highly disproportionate share of economic activity, in spite of significant intra-industry variations, and that firms filing patents differ in many aspects from firms not engaging in patent activity: in particular, they tend to be much larger, require more skilled labor and capital input, and are more productive.

In addition, the nature of innovation seems to be related to the available types of economic activity and the linkages that develop among them. For example, Cai and Li (2012) stress the importance of intersectoral knowledge linkages and the growth-enhancing spillovers that can emerge from networks that connect sectors. Akcigit, Hanley, and Serrano-Velarde (2011) in turn associate the presence of firms in multiple industries with their ability to appropriate cross-industry spillovers and use them as incentives for basic research. This line of thinking accords with the arguments formulated by Hausmann and Hidalgo (2010) and Hausmann and others (2011). They argue that the diversity of economic activities in an economy is crucial for forming collaborations that then allow an economy to climb higher up the product ladder and achieve the ability to competitively offer higher value added products and services. Their indexes rank Greece low on economic diversity and the complexity of the produced export goods, a measure that has been declining since the 1980s.

Numerous studies have described the impediments to competition in Greece. Even though barriers to competition had been extensively documented before 2009 for significant network industries (such as energy and transport) and professional services, the wide range of accumulated smaller or soft impediments across the whole spectrum of economic activity has never been documented systematically by a major research organization or by the official lenders. A recent application of the OECD's Competition Assessment Toolkit (OECD 2013b) to four preselected sectors is one of the few instances where such an attempt has been made. Yet there is sufficient evidence, ranging from administrative cost estimates to the results of perception-based surveys, of a significant problem, one that mainly stems from state-sponsored laws and practices. Notwithstanding the reluctant, partial progress in road haulage, port services, professional services, and reduction of administrative burdens and impediments to competition, there are still many larger and smaller issues that need to be documented and addressed.

The Locus of Technology-Based Innovation Depends on Its Characteristics

The different attributes of various new technologies, and the innovations they can lead to, often depend crucially on the realities of the relevant science and the inevitable gestation process associated with it. The often observed fact that venture capital prefers to invest in software innovations and applications related to social networking (see, for example, Lerner 2012) clearly reflects the reality that such projects have a shorter and more predictable gestation period, from initial conception to initial product placement on the market. In addition, failure in this area usually can be wound down relatively easily and predictably. In contrast, that is not always true for the development of a new, innovative drug that may need decades of research and uncertain and lengthy approval processes before it can reach the market. The same applies to the development of entirely new technologies, such as fiber optics (see Graham 2007). It is also likely that there are many environments in which different types of innovations gestate, and because of the varying conditions of each environment, some innovations are more likely to emerge in smaller companies while others are more likely to emerge in larger ones, as argued by Akcigit and Kerr (2012). Innovations that largely depend on the human capital of a few motivated individuals, such as software for applications, may be more likely to emerge in the flexible environment of smaller enterprises while innovations needing significant capital outlays over a long period of time—especially where expensive infrastructure or basic science is a prerequisite—may require the financial strength offered by larger companies. Jaffe and Lerner (2001) thus specifically stress the long gestation period to move new technologies from initial development stages to final commercialization of the innovation as a very important parameter in the whole process. Graham (2010) argues about the opposing impacts, first, of the reality that innovation has become more scientifically linked, which has increased funding needs, and, second, of the increased flexibility in adapting sizes as physical capital has declined and human capital has increased in importance. Both developments have led to significant changes in the size of the organizations forming innovating networks.

Tellingly, in a 2010 article, *The Economist* argues that the success with which German "Mittelstand" companies target niche markets demonstrates only one of the ways that size and specialization, when adapted to varying circumstances, can lead to success.[3]

The Challenge of Combining All the Necessary Ingredients and the Role of Institutions

Since those who engage in basic research and development usually have backgrounds and skills different from those who introduce innovations into the market, that is, those in business, and since both have backgrounds and skills that differ from those who provide financing—bankers and venture capitalists—there are significant differences in perspective that must be reconciled before successful collaboration among these three groups is possible. Lerner (2007) explicitly identifies problems of entrepreneurs' misgivings about outside investors, that is, those who have built up a company always are suspicious when confronted with outsiders who want to invest in "their" company. The same is undoubtedly true of scientists sharing their life's work with outsiders who will finance and manage the result of their intellectual endeavors and research. Lerner (2007) also describes additional factors that exacerbate this inherent mistrust and can thus undermine the working relationship between the entrepreneur and the finance provider. In considering this dynamic, one must note that the scientists involved are subject to the same understandable human reactions. Aside from uncertainty about possible outcomes, asymmetric information can result from the fact that the investor usually knows less about the business than the entrepreneur, and both of them usually know less than the researcher about the scientific aspects. The resulting mistrust may become even more pronounced when the principal assets are intangibles that are difficult to protect. This is particularly true when rights to the intangibles are insecure or the utilization of such rights depends on the nontransferable personal know-how of one party to the transaction.

Works ranging from Smith (1776) to Graham (2010) stress that sanctity of contract and protection of private property are necessary preconditions for such complicated collaborations. And there are additional critical conditions that must be met. Lerner (2007) stresses that to nurture innovation, there must be a business-friendly environment, readily available legal and other expertise, the ability to leverage the academic and scientific research base in order to encourage technology transfer, conformity with global standards, policies that allow the market to provide direction rather than attempt to steer the market, no crowding out of private initiative by large public programs, and allowance for sufficient flexibility. Other authors such as Baumol and Strom (2010) have shorter lists of prerequisites. The importance of institutions such as the patent system, antitrust law, bankruptcy protection, and the banking system is usually described in such lists. In most cases, however, economists who research this topic conclude that the list of "institutions and things that need to be right" is quite long, which clearly reflects that the whole process of innovation is a seamless interplay of many separate aspects and stages.

In light of the foregoing requirements, especially when sensitive science is involved, opportunities for trade in technology are hampered when participants cannot adequately protect themselves against misappropriation and opportunism. Arora, Ceccagnoli, and Cohen (2007) not only stress the importance of the institutions and practices related to patent process, but they also point to considerations such as increased ability to prevent unintended disclosure and the structure of the innovating organization. Well-defined legal rules and an effective judicial system are also essential in this context (Lerner 2009). Broadly stated, from the perspective of those financing the development of innovation into marketable products or services, any innovation or result of scientific research is only as good as the protection it has at all the stages of development. Thus access to a team with the scientific and legal knowledge to file a good patent and a judicial system that can protect it at a reasonable cost, predictably and with a minimum of delay, is very important.

There are other important issues that should not be ignored. For example, researchers are often not aware of the legal implications of sharing their trade secrets with potential investors, although they must walk a thin line between disclosing enough information to attract investment and revealing so much that it will endanger their intellectual property rights. The same is often true if a researcher has already partnered up with an entrepreneur and they are jointly seeking to attract outside financing. It is thus not surprising that Lerner (2007) points out how the agency problem, which encompasses all these aspects, means that property protection demands a significant degree of flexibility. Only when such flexibility is available can the contracts uniting science, business skills, and financing be adapted on a case-by-case basis.

Lerner (2007) stresses two further preconditions for the success of such collaborations. The parties must be experienced, as otherwise they will not be capable of the sophisticated contracting required for these projects, even if the institutional setting can accommodate such a sophisticated level of contracting. Often this is not the case, as the respective skills of the parties in their own fields do not guarantee a command of the legal, contracting, negotiation, and other skills required at this point. This in turn suggests that professionals with these specialized skills often constitute a crucial part of the team. This not only means inclusion of professionals with the scientific and legal know-how to write good patents but also their presence at the centers where the research is done. Thus legal, business, and accounting support is available to their scientists when they are engaging in discussions with businesses and providers of financing. Effective nondisclosure agreements, contract templates, and advice on how to form companies to hold the intellectual property rights resulting from research—all of these are included in the specialized knowledge that many research centers in developed nations now try to provide to communities that thrive at the juncture of science and business. In many cases the personal talents of university and science center liaison officers responsible for facilitating the relationship between research and business are crucial for successful promotion of collaboration among these communities.

There are also considerations regarding the nature of the entity that will hold the intellectual property and in which all the parties will participate. Research suggests that such an entity should be easy and inexpensive to form and maintain (Bartelsman, Haltiwanger, and Scarpetta 2009). High expenses and cumbersome procedures are obstacles; especially at the early stage of a project, high costs may divert scarce funds from the prime objective, which is to commercialize the science or innovation. The high cost of maintaining the entity also may discourage the development of many other new projects or discourage outside investors from building up portfolios of such projects. Any legal or administrative uncertainty acts as an indirect cost at this stage. Since innovation unavoidably entails a fair amount of failure and the costs thereof, the imposition of additional and avoidable costs will also jeopardize the development of projects that would ultimately be quite successful.

Unfortunately, Greece scores poorly on all of the foregoing preconditions for supporting successful innovation. Start-ups and bankruptcy procedures remain, in spite of numerous attempts at reforms over the past years, surprisingly costly and complicated and are subject to significant legal and administrative uncertainty, even for cases that would be trivial in other countries. Even the sanctity of private contracts is not ensured, as the state often enacts legislation that ignores established practices or provisions affecting important business contracts. Intellectual property rights are difficult to enforce in the slow and sometimes unpredictable Greek courts, and the infrastructure for filing and processing effective patents is weak, largely due to the fact that the profession of patent agent has been relegated to lawyers who basically have no science training. Still, there has been significant progress in some areas. For example, the Hellenic Patent Office has in past years attempted to deal with the numerous shortcomings of the system and to train officers, some initiatives such as the Corallia technology cluster and a number of active research universities and centers have helped to promulgate intellectual property protection and the transfer of legal and financial know-how, and specialized courts for intellectual property adjudication have been established. However, numerous significant shortcomings remain. Furthermore, the expertise that had started to accumulate among the university and science center liaison officers is now being compromised as budget cuts often led to their dismissal.

The Cost of Taxing Success and Punishing Failure

A related and important issue is the tax treatment of the investment in, and returns on, such projects. Lerner (2009) points out the importance of creating tax incentives or at least of removing existing disincentives, arguing that it does matter when tax policies, bankruptcy laws, and related practices in effect tax success and punish failure. Da Rin, Di Giacomo, and Sembenelli (2011) find that corporate taxation exerts an important concave effect on entry rates. They conclude that reductions in taxes have a positive impact on investment levels only once they fall below a certain threshold level. Arnold and Schwellnus (2008) also find that corporate taxes have a negative effect on productivity and reduce investment. They show that the negative effect of corporate taxes is especially pronounced for firms that are catching up with the technological frontier.

Lerner (2009) cites in particular tax flow-through as a practice that is very well adapted to the realities of innovative projects with high uncertainty relative to their outcome, as such a provision makes the partnership effectively invisible for tax purposes. In the optimal case, flow-through taxation also allows the taxable parties to offset gains with losses in other projects, thus reducing the tax burden on the relatively few successful projects that ultimately have to pay the cost of the failures. But these issues go beyond the investors and also affect the parties actively working for the project. While in many countries strategies have emerged that try to adapt to this reality, in many other countries the tax treatment of failure and success leaves little room for experimentation once economic realities and tax law are taken into account.

Both tax law and the adaptability of contract law to the peculiarities of these kinds of complicated collaborations affect flexibility in distributing rewards and limiting losses when the project fails. Lerner (2012) goes so far as to state that compensation schemes must be flexible enough to accommodate seemingly irrational requests from the parties that may not appear to be in their true interest, such as a focus on management fees.

While the formation of an incentives structure appropriate for each case is, as Lerner (2009) argues, the principal way to get an agreement satisfactory to all, there is only one way to effectively protect the parties to the project: limited liability, that is, liability limited to the entity nominally engaging in the project. This is important to protect the scientists from the business and financial risks that they may not be able to gauge accurately or may prefer not to investigate. Limited liability, however, also shields business partners and silent investors from unfamiliar risks inherent in scientific projects. In many countries the legal entities offering limited liability may be costly to form or maintain; in other cases they may not offer the tax advantages of other legal entities that do not offer limited liability. Similarly, the legal entities offering advantageous tax treatment may not permit freely transferable shares, an attribute that may be limited to more expensive legal forms. Yet all of these attributes are desirable to ensure a contract structure will be able to satisfy all parties and also reassure them that they will have a large degree of flexibility in their future commitments to the proposed project. The latter is crucial because the fast-changing exigencies for each project often require the ability to change the ownership structure easily, on short notice and without unreasonable expense.

Compared with the question of adequately compensating success, the issue of managing failure is often overlooked. But Aghion and others (2008) argue that exit costs also are an important consideration for innovative companies. They also argue that stringent employment protection reduces observable patterns of firm behavior associated with experimentation and, as expected, reduces firm-level employment volatility. The same argument is made by Bravo Biosca (2010), who also stresses the importance of growth and decline, and documents that Europe has many more static firms compared to the United States. He argues that this pattern indicates that in Europe there is less experimentation and a slower reallocation of resources from less to more productive businesses, both of which are important for growth in productivity. Bravo Biosca concludes that policies to facilitate the formation of high-growth companies must be matched by deeper structural reforms that remove not only barriers to entry but also barriers to adapting to the consequences of growth and contraction. These would entail improving product and labor market regulation, enabling access to finance, and reducing the European market fragmentation that prevents businesses, especially in the service industries, from operating across borders.

In Greece flow-through taxation is not available for entities that offer limited liability and low maintenance costs. Worse still, as a result of recent changes in the law, limited liability for company obligations to the state has essentially been abolished for all officers of a limited liability company, which may seriously discourage scientists from becoming officers in such companies. Furthermore, the taxation of high-risk endeavors in particular is inconsistent and incongruous as a result of the notoriously frequent, unpredictable, and haphazard changes in the tax laws, decrees, circulars, and related implementation practices.

The general complexity and opacity of the tax laws and tax system in Greece often generate specific obstacles to innovation. For instance, until recently R&D expenditures were not even recognized as such by the Greek tax authorities. In many cases simply departing from established business practices may lead to serious problems. For example, the pure alcohol used to filter residue from the production of olive oil is taxed as a beverage, thus making a certain innovative process economically infeasible in Greece. A related project is now being implemented in Sweden rather than in Crete exactly because of this counterproductive regulation. In a different arena, an effort to license a laboratory in Greece to perform acute medical tests related to an innovative method for heart surgery failed due to obstacles imposed by the licensing process; the tests, along with their budget and intellectual property, now have been transferred to the United Kingdom.

Finally, winding down failed business initiatives is notoriously complicated and expensive in Greece: the World Bank's Doing Business index shows that most of the remaining value of assets is destroyed in the process, and the OECD (2013a) documents how significantly the fear of failure inhibits business initiatives in the country.[4]

Basic Research: Infrastructure, Transfer of Knowledge, and the Role of the State

Since the centers engaged in basic research are largely funded, directly or indirectly, by the Greek government, the extent to which the government should have a claim on the resultant intellectual property is an issue. A useful response comes from the Bayh-Dole Act: allowing the private sector to benefit from the transfer of this kind of knowledge is, in effect, the best subsidy that the state can offer to the private sector.[5] The Bayh-Dole Act of 1980 is cited by Jaffe and Lerner (2001), Lerner (2007), Hausman (2012), and Graham (2010) as an important change that facilitated the transfer of knowledge and technologies out of the laboratory and into the national economy via private investment. This act is credited with enhancing the access of business to the key innovation networks within the United States. Furthermore, it gave universities automatic title to the research performed at their institutions—despite being funded by the federal government—which meant that they no longer needed to go through complicated and lengthy government procedures to obtain licenses for the technologies they developed. The positive effect of this act on innovation in the United States demonstrates that there is a real need to make it easier for research institutions to license their technologies.

The impact of this act, as well as the legends surrounding Silicon Valley, often give the impression that, except for the formation of appropriate supporting institutions, the role of the government should be one of absence rather than the promotion of policy through project initiatives. Further support for this assessment can be found in multiple examples. Lerner (2009) cites numerous cases in which ill-designed government programs have squandered untold amounts of taxpayer money with little to show for it. Lerner (2007) also provides evidence that government grants do not tend to finance the kind of R&D that leads to tangible innovations. Darby and Zucker (2007) show that for American biotech start-ups, there is no positive correlation between receiving government grants and the ability to successfully go public as a company. On the other hand, success in going public is associated with the publication record of scientists that participate as officers in the company or work for the start-up as well as with the ability to prepare patent applications and attract venture capital.

Yet there are also valid counterarguments relating to government's role. Lerner (2009) notes that even though government grants do not create tangible results, they have stimulated the development of a knowledge base for support services, ranging from law to accounting, and helped companies that received earlier government grants to succeed later with other projects. Furthermore, Jaffe and Lerner (2001) note the important role of procurement programs in the formation of industry structure and technology diffusion. Fabrizio and Mowery (2007) argue that government-funded programs were critical in establishing the initial conditions for industry evolution that influenced subsequent firm strategies and industry structures. Lerner (2009) also stresses that many of the firms initially forming the core of Silicon Valley relied on government-financed projects. Similarly, Hausman (2012) argues that counties surrounding universities that received federal funding—particularly from the Department of Defense and the National Institutes of Health—experienced faster employment growth after the Bayh-Dole Act was passed. Thus she argues that, as an illustration of their complementarity with universities, large establishments contributed substantially more to the total twenty-year growth effect than did small establishments. And Kitson and Michie (forthcoming) argue the need for government programs to support the development of science and technology clusters. On that point Audretsch, Hülsbeck, and Lehmann (2012) point out that while regional competitiveness and university spillovers have complementary effects on the innovative behavior of firms, some of this positive influence may be mitigated by possible crowding-out effects. This illustrates the complicated nature of the relationships between state-financed research institutions and an innovative business community.

It should be added that the nurturing of an environment that can support research and provide it with an outlet to the markets seems to require the existence of a healthy manufacturing base, as suggested for example by McKinsey (2012b), the World Economic Forum (2013), and Locke and Wellhausen (2014). The documented interdependence between manufacturing and services, both as inputs and as demand between each, implies that even the ability of the service sector to move higher up the value chain seems to require at some stages the coexistence with some sophisticated and basic manufacturing. And manufacturing in turn appears to need a link with centers that conduct primary research—the "R" in R&D—as a crucial component in its ability to innovate.

It is in this sense that the innovation infrastructure and the remaining manufacturing capacity of Greece are important assets whose survival needs to be ensured. Support for these potential drivers of long-term growth will create a demand for a highly skilled workforce (Rodrik, Hausmann, and Hwang 2006) and should complement and advance the natural comparative advantage of Greece in areas such as tourism, shipping, and agricultural production.

To repeat an earlier observation, Greek research universities and centers, financed through the government and EU structural funds, have achieved a quantitative and qualitative level that stands out with respect to the other measures of innovation and research performance in the country. And yet there are numerous institutional obstacles faced by these universities and centers when they desire to collaborate with the private sector. Therefore the long-established tradition of eschewing contact with business and seeking either more government financing or projects financed by EU funds has persisted even though government financing has become increasingly scarce given the present financial difficulties of the Greek government.

The following is a list of some major obstacles to research–private sector collaboration in Greece as of this writing:

—Researchers in public universities (that is, all Greek research universities) are not allowed to participate in companies as shareholders or officers. This either-or situation is an impediment to innovative collaboration when researchers must choose to leave an established academic career for a start-up with high risk of failure at an early stage or if they desire to combine both activities.

—Research that leads to successful start-ups or lucrative patents does not count toward academic advancement.

—Permission to license research results obtained at a government-funded institution or permission for a government-funded institution to receive a grant from a company for research work or for the purchase inputs has to be obtained from governing boards that are still in some cases influenced by individuals opposed to the collaboration of business and academia.

—The law that prescribes the rights of the institution to license intellectual property is vague. Ostensibly the institution could do so indirectly through the setting up of separate research centers. However, due to these ambiguities, the governing boards, which make the decision to permit licensing, almost never act for fear of being accused of selling out.

Some improvements were attempted with a law during 2012. For example, research centers, but not universities, can confer academic rewards on researchers who initiate successful start-ups; researchers from these centers can leave for a few years to work in such start-ups; and it has become easier to license intellectual property to such start-ups. However, soft and hard opposition to cooperation with the private sector remains at major research universities while reform of the governance of these institutions lately has been reversed and now suffers from the lack of a clear and decisive strategy.

Furthermore, it should be stressed that Greek manufacturing, the natural outlet for a high percentage of R&D-driven innovation, has suffered for decades from the relative disadvantage, compared with services, of the irrational, unpredictable, and corrupt licensing process and the high uncertainty of the often surreal public policies and tax laws and practices. The latter disproportionally hurt manufacturing, which entails high up-front investments that are depreciated over many years. The resulting deterioration of the Greek manufacturing base has seriously diminished a key outlet for research results and simultaneously degraded the business and knowledge environment, as reflected in the quality of the mix of exported goods (see Hausmann and others 2011). It must be stressed at this point that important reforms have been implemented in the licensing process, and when completed they are expected to lead to significant improvements.

Financing

The OECD (2011c) states that access to finance for new and innovative small firms involves both debt and equity financing. Even before the recent financial crisis, banks were reluctant to lend to small and young firms. It remains the case that large companies with established cash flow are less expensive to screen for financing eligibility, both in terms of human labor and cost and as a fraction of the bank financing made available. In contrast, small and young businesses traditionally have a high turnover rate, and therefore to the extent that they cannot offer hard collateral, as is usually the case, they are a very high risk for a bank. This problem is amplified for young and small businesses engaged in innovative projects: loan officers are hampered in their risk assessment of such projects by the lack of standardized benchmarks. This problem is exacerbated when the enterprise involves pioneering, cutting-edge research, given the absence of comparative benchmarks and the fact that bank officials do not have the requisite scientific knowledge to assess such projects—nor is it part of their job to have such a background.

Small innovative businesses are more costly, per euro or dollar of loan issued, to screen and monitor, and their focus on innovation means higher levels of uncertainty and risks. Such realities imply that these kinds of companies are not as fit for standardized bulk bank financing as are other, more predictable activities undertaken by established companies with a proven track record. This observation points to the often over-looked fact that the financing of innovative projects is essentially incompatible with the core business of banks as a result of their inherently different missions. Therefore alternative sources of funds, from angel investors for the initial stages of a project to venture capitalists for projects that have survived some initial tests, are critical to ensure financing tailor-made for small innovative initiatives. It needs to be stressed that just as the financing profile for well-established activities differs from the financing profile for innovative initiatives, so does the financing profile differ according to size of the business; this means that the financing profile of small noninnovative firms differs from that of small innovative firms. As shown in multiple examples mentioned in various chapters of Lamoreaux and Sokoloff (2007), it is no coincidence that larger companies tend to finance their own innovative projects with the internal cash flow generated from established business lines that, unsurprisingly, benefit from bank financing.

The importance of alternative financing for innovative, young, small initiatives should not be measured according to their small size, in relation to the entities that constitute the bulk of bank and other financing within the economy. Size in this context is not the critical factor. The preponderance of economic activities entail established practices, regardless of the scale of the business. Globally this means billions of people go to the same jobs every day where they more or less do the same thing they did the day before, and the stable and repetitive activities of their employers are financed by traditional loan and equity financing. But every day a small fraction of these activities is terminated and a small fraction of new activities springs up. While the former are recorded as equity losses or covered by bad loan provisions of the banks, the latter often require financing that does not fit the traditional standardized bulk-financing business. As Lerner (2007) points out, a significant degree of flexibility is needed in the financing structure for these new, often disparate enterprises. And although the availability of flexible, nonstandard financing is critical to the survival of such small start-ups, it would constitute only a tiny fraction of the demand for loan products within a given economy. In this context the emergence and institutionalization of the venture capital industry have been key developments. But overall they need to be seen as specific examples of a need for broader evolution of financial services, one that continuously tries to adapt to the changing requirements of a small fraction of the total business population whose financing needs do not fit the standard template of bulk financing. This area of financial innovation is prone to excesses and failures exactly because of its often near experimental nature. However, any attempt to regulate it away and allocate this function to state-sponsored schemes that imitate the bulk financing paradigm to cover financing needs of innovative startups and projects will most likely fail to replicate the success even if it avoids any particular failures.

Another key point to understand is that these marginal but crucially important, nonstandardized financing methods can only exist in an environment where bulk financing is healthy and has a harmonious relationship with the majority of a business population that is also healthy and diverse, both with respect to size and activities. This point is of particular importance in the aftermath of the recent global financial crisis because numerous policymakers seem to envision both a stringently regulated and heavily taxed financial services sector and broad, preferably state-sponsored, financing schemes that will support a spate of innovative businesses, even in low-growth economies operating in an environment of highly compromised debt and equity markets.

In Greece the difficulty in financing innovation is just another challenge adding to the cumulative burden of aforementioned obstacles. Collectively they further discourage collaboration between businesses and the state-sponsored research institutions. Ironically, since Greek policymakers traditionally associate innovation only with small companies and accordingly have shaped an institutional environment that has been hostile toward larger companies for decades, they may have actively discouraged innovation in Greece given that smaller innovative businesses are especially dependent on outside financing and access to the research facilities of others. In addition, the latest regulatory developments in Europe, which encourage a deleveraging of financial intermediation with the aim of reducing systematic risks, create a situation where business initiatives will face stiffer bank lending conditions even while they do not have ready access to alternatives (unlike larger companies that can tap into the corporate bond market). The particular challenges of the banking system in Greece, described in chapter 2, are amplified for smaller innovative Greek companies. A comprehensive policy response would have to deal with numerous issues, ranging from creating possible corporate bond markets for smaller companies, with less costly terms of participation, to creating a framework for securitization to increasing the level of flexibility in the conduct of such financing deals.

Evidence provided by the OECD (2011c) shows that more than half of business R&D usually originates from large companies. However, because of the extreme policy bias toward small companies, the Greek corporate landscape is now characterized by an exceptionally low average company size.[6] This means that Greece has been deprived of significant contributions to business R&D simply because of its hostility toward larger companies, which would have the ability to internally finance R&D, especially more demanding research activities. As the remaining possible contributors to business R&D in Greece, the smaller companies by definition are more dependent on outside financing if they want to undertake such initiatives and therefore are subject to the aforementioned challenges of dealing with the bulk financing system (see Bain and Institute of International Finance 2013). An associated issue is the lack of physical infrastructure in which to conduct R&D. Establishing in-house facilities is an economically viable option only for large or exceptional companies. But the small size of most Greek companies means that if they want to engage in R&D and even if they can secure financing, they will most likely need access to others' facilities to conduct their research. Their main option in Greece is often to collaborate with government-sponsored research facilities at universities and state-run science parks—the very entities that shun or forbid collaboration with business, or at least did in the past. The OECD (2011c) has found that the bulk of business R&D expenditure is for personnel costs; given this situation, the significant difficulty of engaging researchers to work on business-related projects in government-sponsored research institutions seems to have added yet another obstacle in the path of Greek companies seeking to innovate and conduct R&D.

Firm Size and Age: How They Relate to Innovation and Employment

Not all types of technology development and innovation follow similar paths until they reach the market. Furthermore, innovation in various companies depends upon their size, their age, and many other characteristics. That means that the realities of all these companies and the preconditions for their success and ability to innovate often differ significantly. This array of different routes to innovation contrasts with the frequent attempt to seek simplifying stereotypes for innovation, especially when designing public policy. Tellingly, recent research clarifies the fallacy of the frequent misconception that innovation is associated with small companies. This fallacy is even more relevant to our analysis, as it stresses once again the difficulty of obtaining data sets that fully document firm dynamics and the inevitability that such studies fail to present the full extent of the dynamics of growth and attrition that exists in reality. Yet, as data sets have improved, at least in some countries, there now seems to be sufficient evidence to support the thesis that it is a company's age, rather than its size, that determines its association with innovation. For example, De Kok and others (2011) state that SMEs create more jobs than large enterprises, but they do not include in their sample shrinking SMEs, which obviously introduces a significant bias in their analysis. The findings of Haltiwanger, Jarmin, and Miranda (2009) are more directly relevant. They point out the importance of entry and post-entry dynamics for young firms. The authors use a novel data set to track private nonagricultural business start-ups in the United States on a comprehensive basis. They document the critical role of job creation by start-ups in determining aggregate job creation by the business economy. They also find that while the rate of job creation in small firms is much higher than that in larger firms, aggregate job creation remains comparable among the groups of smaller and larger companies. Also, while the surviving firms are found to grow very fast and to have above-average productivity, the employment-weighted exit rate of firms is also much higher for young firms. The exiting firms are also less productive. The point made by this analysis is that the extent to which a country exhibits patterns of both static and dynamic efficiency will depend on its market structure and institutions, and both are important parts of the process that shifts resources away from less productive to more productive activities. In the end any size effects disappear once the age of the firm is controlled for, which highlights the importance of young firms, and in particular start-ups, for job creation as part of a healthy economy that allows the new to take hold.

Lerner (2009) deals with the relationship between size, innovation, and age of companies and comes to a parallel conclusion that youth, rather than size, is a decisive factor for innovation. Meanwhile Stangler and Litan (2009) argue that the characteristic of firm age, not necessarily size, is the driver of job creation. The fact is that most young firms tend to be smaller. Still, the data show that even while young (and thus often smaller) companies are found to contribute the lion's share of new jobs, older and larger companies still matter for job growth, and that is not only because their smaller rates of job creation are applied to a much larger number of employees but also because they are able to finance and support different innovations that require resources that the smaller and younger companies simply cannot muster. Thus the authors conclude that their U.S. data demonstrate a symbiotic relationship between young and mature firms of all sizes.

Ultimately, the simplistic idea that innovative activity should be associated with size distracts once again from the intuitive understanding that the rich and versatile landscape of innovation implies that there are many different paths that lead to innovation, in companies of all types and sizes. All these companies have different needs in different areas, and catering to the needs related to one such area does not mean that needs in another area should be neglected. In the end, all these needs represent necessary components of a healthy business ecosystem that favors innovation across the board, a proposition compatible with the findings of the OECD (2011a).

The importance of young start-ups does not alter the fact that the bulk of employment is in jobs that repeat practices of the past and in companies that slowly adopt innovations as they adjust to changing realities.

Though research centers generate a lot of knowledge, only a small part of it finds its way into the production of goods and services and thus into general society. Yet the large body of knowledge that has no immediate application in the innovation of products and processes is a prerequisite for the attempts and failures that ultimately lead to innovative products and services or the components that make these possible. This small fraction of all R&D that trickles into innovations can have an impact far wider than its narrow contribution. The improvements in ICT, logistics, and supply chain management in the United States in the 1990s are a good example of the potential scope of effects. These wide-ranging effects in turn create the opportunities that new companies of all sizes and older, restructuring companies can take advantage of and thereby generate new jobs.

The skewed distribution in favor of small companies hints at the reality that the private sector in Greece is not allowed to form the aforementioned healthy pattern of diverse coexisting companies that is the prerequisite of a well-functioning business ecosystem. In the final analysis, Greece's dismal performance with respect to business R&D and employment expenditure before the crisis despite its predominance of small firms constitutes per se proof that the existence of large numbers of small companies is not a sufficient condition for fostering innovation and creating jobs.

Contributors to Business R&D Expenditure: A Quantitative Investigation

Having identified factors that encourage business R&D expenditure and compared them to the challenges described from interviews in Greece, we apply quantitative analysis to evaluate the relevance of the issues identified. In particular, we seek to establish with available data which aspects of the institutional environment in which businesses operate are related to their decision to invest in R&D. The results of this analysis are then compared with the findings of the literature and the interviews.

Data Collection

The preceding description of Greek performance in research and innovation relies on the numerous factors that the literature has shown to affect companies' innovative activity, especially more demanding research-based initiatives, as well as on extensive interviews conducted in Greece. However, the quantitative impact of these factors on business-financed

R&D—which occurs at a particularly low level in Greece—has yet to be examined. Therefore this section investigates that relationship, and in particular the question as to whether low R&D expenditure by Greek companies is the result of their customary and voluntary usages and practices or the outcome of the institutional and business environment created by official policy.

Thus we sought data for the purpose of quantifying, in a compatible data set, the factors and parameters identified in the aforementioned literature. We selected variables that reflected the parameters mentioned, keeping in mind the significant challenges of this approach, some of which are described by Wunsch-Vincent (2012).

The difficulties in collecting compatible data from a sufficiently comprehensive set of countries and years increase if one seeks to include qualitative aspects of innovative businesses. This would entail distinguishing between innovation based on R&D—especially research—and other types of innovation by analyzing hard evidence on business and research community collaboration, such as jointly filed patents, employment schemes, and IPOs of university spin-offs. Alternatively, one can focus (as we do) on business R&D expenditure that covers only the more demanding innovative activity that stems from R&D and does not measure innovative activity not related directly to R&D, despite the relatively comprehensive and reliable data available about the latter. There is a potential for distortion when analyzing only a proxy for a part of all innovation activity, for instance, when process and product line innovation in a given environment flourishes even while R&D-based innovation does not. However, this distortion should be lessened by the fact that good performance in R&D innovation generally will reflect a dynamic and healthy environment in which the other methods of innovation also find fertile ground. Furthermore, given our particular interest in the potential benefits of better linkage between research centers and the business community, the emphasis on this particular kind of innovative activity is justified.

Figures for business expenditure on R&D (BERD), along with government, university, and nonprofit expenditure on R&D, are available for the countries covered by Eurostat. Similar data are available for OECD member countries, as well as some other nonmember countries covered by the OECD database. To the extent that the same countries appear in both databases, their data coincide. Still, the number of countries covered in both data sets is only a fraction of the total number of countries globally and includes only developed countries that are privileged members of the European Union and the OECD. Similar data can be sourced for most countries from United Nations (UN) databases. But the high correlation (shown in appendix B, figure 1) of the Eurostat–OECD data for BERD with the respective perception index used by the World Economic Forum Global Competitiveness Report suggests that a reliable analysis can be performed on the basis of the latter, especially given the fact that the WEF GCR contains subindexes that cover numerous issues relevant to our analysis and thus readily provide us with a consistent data set for almost all countries. This is especially true since the latest update of the WEF database provides a level of conformity and compatibility that would be difficult to reproduce at this stage of the investigation. The exact methodology and the sources for each subindex are provided by the WEF in detail as part of its annual GCR report. The main reservation about the use of this data set is that it is generally based on a perceptions survey of representatives of the business community in the countries covered. The responses come from about eighty survey participants in each country; the sample is stratified into larger and smaller companies and into repeat and new participants. Although such perception surveys have been criticized, especially by political leaders in countries with unfavorable rankings, this does not change the fact that the survey responses tend to correlate highly with indexes based on hard evidence, such as the World Bank's Doing Business report, and hard data, such as business expenditure on R&D. A related analysis of the arguments and literature in support of the positive contribution from the use of such indexes—while admitting their limitations—is provided by the Hellenic Federation of Enterprises (2007), which cites, among others, the work of Rose-Ackerman (2006).

The subjectivity associated with subindexes based on the perceptions of a small sample of the business community implies a related concern about measurement errors; however, for the purpose of our investigation and given the size of the dataset, this poses a nonvital problem for the analysis. The data set also includes subindexes from the World Bank WGI, since they constitute a comprehensive data set for a large number of countries about characteristics of governance that are a priori potential explanatory variables. The selected variables focus on measures compatible with areas identified in the literature as potentially critical for the encouragement of innovative business activity. While not all issues raised in the literature could be associated with a given measure, and some are not represented, or are only broadly represented, by some metrics, all the following key areas are covered: financing, institutions, property protection, labor relations, competition, health of business environment as reflected by the span of value chains, educational quality, and research capacity (see table 3-2). Although certain attributes evaluated by Doing Business, such as procedures for company start-ups or bankruptcy, are not explicitly represented in the proposed list, the performance of countries with respect to such attributes tends to be highly correlated with other broader measures that are included, such as the quality of governance.

The data set for the selected variables covered the period from 2007 to 2011, years with the largest number of countries having data. It should be noted that Albania and Vietnam were ultimately excluded from the data set because they appeared to be outliers, probably as a result of rapid improvement in some indexes during the brief time range covered. It should also be noted that since the performance of most countries stayed relatively stable during years selected, the time dimension was suppressed in the analysis; related robustness checks for selected individual years demonstrated no visible impact on the results of the analysis, and the resulting increased sample size was used for the benefit of the quantitative analysis. Scatter plots of all involved variables, as well as a number of other variables, were visually inspected for the entire 2007–11 period as well as for selected years, and for subgroups of countries (jointly OECD and EU members, and nonmembers); changes among these in the correlations for the selection of subgroups were identified; and points that stood out were also identified in order to juxtapose them and to avoid potential errors in the data analysis.

It should be stressed here that the WEF GCR variable measuring industry-university collaboration was not included among the potential dependent variables. This follows as a result of its very high correlation with the variable that measures BERD, as shown in the appendix B, figure 2, as well as the fact that, like BERD, it is tantamount to a candidate-dependent variable. For the same reason, the variable of cluster development also was not included among the potential dependent variables, despite its obvious relevance. Again, the strong and positive correlation between BERD and cluster development (appendix B, figure 3) enables the exclusion of the latter variable. This decision is further supported by the finding of McKinsey (2012b) that company R&D spending, and in particular the research expenditure, often is realized by the financing of activities located in such clusters and centers, implying that the causality between the two variables is probably bidirectional and that the same

Table 3-2. *Candidate Regressors and Dependent Variable*

Variables	Subindexes or indicators
	WEF GCR (1–7 best)
Dependent	12.03 Company spending on R&D
Independent	
1	1.01 Property rights
2	1.02 Intellectual property protection
3	1.09 Burden of government regulation
4	2.01 Quality of overall infrastructure
5	5.03 Quality of the educational system
6	6.01 Intensity of local competition
7	6.13 Burden of customs procedures
8	7.02 Flexibility of wage determination
9	8.05 Venture capital availability
10	10.01 Domestic market size index
11	11.05 Value chain breadth
12	12.02 Quality of scientific research institutions
	World Bank Governance Indicators (estimate)
13	Control of corruption
14	Government effectiveness
15	Regulatory quality
16	Rule of law
17	Voice and accountability

Sources: World Economic Forum, "Global Competitiveness Report" (www.weforum.org/issues/global-competitiveness); World Bank, "Worldwide Governance Indicators" (http://info.worldbank.org/governance/wgi/index.aspx#home).

factors that encourage BERD also encourage the development of such clusters through BERD, rather than exclusively through the public funds made available for their development.

Data Analysis

As expected, strong multicollinearity among the initial full set of suggested exogenous independent variables emerged as an immediate problem. The high correlation among numerous variables in the data set is a reasonable consequence of the fact that countries that have reached higher levels of institutional maturity tend to score high on many of the issues covered by the selected variables. This strong multicollinearity tends to confirm the thinking of Rodrik (2007) that developed nation status can be achieved only once all pieces of the puzzle are in place, irrespective of the fact that periods of growth can be achieved by freeing up specific bottlenecks in some developing economies. Still, the correlations among the different variables of the initial data set suggest some particularly strong and interesting associations.

The near-zero determinant of the covariance matrix with all candidate exogenous variables, appropriately adjusted for their means, and the often very high vector inflation factors and near-zero eigenvalues provided further proof of the extent of multicollinearity. The initial analysis of the full set of candidate exogenous variables also revealed additional textbook symptoms of multicollinearity such as a high R^2 but insignificant individual t statistics that in turn are highly dependent on the given specification of the model (see, among others, Greene 2007; Judge and others 1982).

The elimination of variables—a potential remedy suggested by Greene (2007)—is not as onerous in this particular context as it may be in others. The reason is that taking note of the abovementioned correlations permits us to interpret the results of any regressions based on a reduced selection of variables as proof that the factors measured by such variables remain significant in the aggregate. While this will not allow us to identify the specific influence of all individual candidate-independent variables, it will still permit us to draw some general conclusions about the aggregate importance of the level of institutional development and permit qualified conclusions about differences among countries in light of their development status.

The elimination from the list of available candidate exogenous variables follows initially from the identification of those variables with the largest vector inflation factors (over 3) and until the determinant of the matrix with the independent variables reaches a value that is not too close to zero. For each elimination of a variable, we checked whether it had large correlations with other variables and whether its elimination had a visible impact on the increase on the determinant of the correlation matrix of the exogenous variables, its characteristic roots, and the other vector inflation factors (of the inverse correlation matrix). The resulting specification of the reduced data set no longer suffered from the symptoms of extreme multicollinearity. Subsequent elementary tests, such as the Breusch-Pagan test and the Goldfeld-Quandt test on the one-third of the sample with the highest ranks in government effectiveness (which contains most OECD and EU member states) and the one-third of the bottom performers, and an observation of the ordinary least squares (OLS) residuals immediately revealed significant heteroscedasticity. The process of dealing with multicollinearity already alerted us to the fact that our simple specification to describe a much more complicated reality would likely suffer from misspecifications such as omitted variables, measurement errors, and incorrect functional forms; therefore heteroscedasticity was not only expected but interpreted as a very likely indication of other problems, such as the ones just mentioned (see Judge and others 1982). When the sample was sorted into three subgroups of countries according to the level of government effectiveness (see appendix B, table 1), with the highest performing countries included in tier 1 and the lowest performing countries in tier 3, the performance of separate OLS regressions for each of the three subgroups revealed widespread heteroscedasticity among each subgroup, as well as some important differences in the estimates of some of the parameters of the model and the explanatory power of the given specification. The indication of different constants and, in particular, of some slope coefficients for each subgroup motivated us to apply the "seemingly unrelated regression model," which revealed near-zero off-diagonal elements of the estimated covariance matrix. This outcome led to the decision to examine each subgroup separately.

In appendix B, tables 2a through 2c display the correlations of the variables included in the regressor matrix for each subgroup (tier) of countries. Appendix B, table 3, lists the averages and the standard deviations for each variable in each subgroup and in Greece. It should be noted that in appendix table 3 the averages evolve in expected ways; only the index on wage flexibility does not exhibit the expected worsening in the lower tiers of the separated data.

For each subgroup OLS regressions were performed for the complete set of independent variables, and the already described elimination strategy was followed for each subgroup. Then, based on a new examination of the correlations among the full set of candidate exogenous variables for each subgroup, some iterations were used to test robustness. The repetition of this process revealed some interesting facts in the sense that the correlations that had appeared in the complete data set seemed to be driven in some cases by the strong correlation for each of the three specific subgroups.

The following indicative significant (positive) correlations are presented in appendix B, tables 2a through 2c:

—Property rights and intellectual property rights correlate with government effectiveness, rule of law, control of corruption, burden of customs procedures, and regulatory quality among tier 1 countries. These correlations also exist among the tier 2 and tier 3 countries, but some are weaker. Control of corruption also has many other strong correlations in all tiers.

—Quality of infrastructure is correlated with government effectiveness in tier 1 and tier 2 countries, with the breadth of the value chain in tier 1 and tier 3 countries and the burden of customs procedures in tier 3 countries.

—The quality of education is correlated with the control of corruption and the effectiveness of government in the tier 1 subgroup.

—The intensity of local competition is correlated with the control of corruption, the effectiveness of government and regulatory quality in the tier 3 subgroup, and the breadth of the value chain and the quality of research institutions in all three tiers, but strongest in tier 3. In addition, intensity of local competition also has a stronger correlation with the protection of property and intellectual property among the tier 2 and 3 subgroups.

—Availability of venture capital funds is highly correlated with property rights and the protection of intellectual property rights in tiers 1 and 2 but less so in tier 3. This may imply that in developing countries other informal contracts that do not depend on official institutions may also develop.

The high correlation among many variables that reflect the "aggregate" level of development of an economy among the first tier countries seems to reaffirm the interpretation that achieving the status of developed nation is a complex process resulting from a multitude of factors.

The Breusch-Pagan test for each subgroup and the inspection of the OLS residuals were used to reaffirm, for each separate specification, the extent of heteroscedasticity for each case cleared of multicollinearity, as had been done for the complete data set initially. We attempted to deal with the problem through a correction based on a restriction that assumed that the disturbances were a function of some of the exogenous variables. This approach led to a visible improvement, as reflected in the examination of the disturbances obtained from the feasible generalized least square estimation (FGLS), in particular when the adjustment of the FGLS was appropriately based on the separate regression of the logarithm of the variance estimator, which in turn was based on the OLS errors, on a constant and the variable selected for each subgroup (venture capital accessibility for tiers 1 and 3, and government effectiveness for tier 2). Furthermore, in this specification the parameter estimates changed little when compared with the OLS regression, while the standard errors changed significantly, leading overall to much increased *t* statistic values that are compatible with very high significance levels. A simpler specification, based on a regression of the variance estimator on a constant and the mentioned variable of each subgroup, was not adopted because it reduced the heteroscedasticity in the residuals visibly less. The high dependence of the variance estimators on the exogenous variable used in each case suggests that the root of the heteroscedasticity problem was indeed the dependence of the residuals on the regressors, itself a reasonable result of our attempt to force on the complex realities of the development process such a simple model that uses aggregated variables. The results of the three separate regressions, for each subgroup, are presented in appendix B, table 4 (regressions 1, 2, and 3). A number of additional tests, such as for the symmetry and kurtosis of the disturbances, were also performed.

Interpretation of Data Analysis

The following describes the results of the FGLS regressions on the three separate groups.

Among the tier 1 countries, availability of venture capital funds, value chain breadth, and the quality of research institutions remained as explanatory variables with statistical significance at the 0.01 level and with high positive coefficients, while the educational system remained at the 0.05 level and the flexibility of wages (with a small coefficient) at the 0.1 level. These variables are in turn highly correlated with the variables of property rights, protection of intellectual property rights, rule of law, government effectiveness, and control of corruption—a relationship that implies that the latter variables remain important in spite of their removal for the sake of reducing multicollinearity, but we are not able to separate their impact using our specification.

For the tier 2 countries, the variables of burden of government regulation, intensity of local competition, venture capital availability, value chain breadth, and quality of research institutions had positive and relatively high coefficients with significance at the 0.01 level. Infrastructure and wage flexibility, at the same significance level, have nevertheless negative and much smaller—as an absolute number—coefficients, while regulatory quality has a much larger—as an absolute number—negative coefficient. The quality of the educational system, again with a negative coefficient, is significant at the 0.1 level. These variables are in turn highly correlated with the variables of property rights, protection of intellectual property rights, burden of customs, government effectiveness, rule of law, and voice and accountability—variables that had been removed to reduce multicollinearity.

For the tier 3 countries, the quality of the educational system, the intensity of local competition, venture capital availability, value chain breadth, and the quality of scientific research institutions are significant at the 0.01 level and have high and positive coefficients. Market size, with a small positive coefficient, and the burden of government regulation, with a small negative coefficient, are significant at the 0.05 level, and the flexibility of wage determination has a small negative coefficient at the 0.1 level. These variables are in turn highly correlated with the variables of property rights, protection of intellectual property rights, customs procedures, government effectiveness, regulatory quality, and the rule of law.

The extent to which these variables are correlated with the other candidate regressors also offers insights. Property rights, protection of intellectual property rights, government effectiveness, the rule of law, and regulatory quality (with some interesting negative—even if small—correlations, especially in tier 2 countries) all appear highly correlated in all three subgroups with regressors that remain in the specification, thus suggesting that these indexes are related to the indexes measured as important for business R&D. In view of the above, the importance of a high-quality research infrastructure, specialized financing, and a broad value chain emerge as key ingredients for the R&D activity of the private sector. Furthermore, the intensity of local competition also emerges as important for the two lower tiers of our data set—possibly because it is a given for the OECD, EU, and Commonwealth member states that basically constitute the first tier of our data set. Overall, the robust importance of competitive markets and a broad value chain corroborate both the literature that argues in favor of competitive markets and the literature that stresses the importance of a versatile production base in the economy.

It has to be noted that tier 2 is the only case in which one of the WB WGI variables, the estimate for regulatory quality, emerged as significant in the regression and with a negative coefficient. Only in this tier is this variable negatively correlated with the WEF variables for burden of government regulation, quality of educational system, and venture capital availability, and it is the only case where regulatory quality remains significant at the 0.01 level. While these negative correlations may go toward explaining the negative coefficient in this particular group, one should also consider that the given variable captures the "ability of the government to formulate and implement sound policies and regulations that permit and promote private sector development."[7] Thus, especially for countries that are midway between the most and least developed, the evaluation of the intent of government and the still prevailing reality— for example, with regard to the burden of regulation or the quality of the educational system—may indeed differ significantly. The fact that in all alternatives the variable for burden of government regulation has the expected sign, and with high significance, goes toward supporting this interpretation.

The correlation between the level of competition and the breadth of the value chain, along with the significance of both variables in tiers 2 and 3, should also be noted, especially since it appears to reflect the significance of competition to the development of a healthy upstream economy. Competition thus appears to benefit the very structure of the whole economy, beyond any impact on consumer prices—which is usually cited as the prime policy objective in political discourse. Furthermore, the significance of both the intensity of competition and the quality of research institutions seems to affirm the view expressed in the literature that competition drives companies to innovate, and that in the case of R&D innovation— and especially research-based innovation—this requires an association with high-quality research institutions.

Another variable that merits a comment is flexibility of wages. While it achieves high significance only in tier 2, it has a positive sign only in tier 1, and in all cases the absolute size of the coefficient is small. Still, if the issue of significance is set aside, the value of the parameter seems to increase as a country reaches higher development levels. With the cautionary note that the issue of wage flexibility may be affected by complicated relationships and nonlinearities that depend on a broad context (see Nicoletti and Scarpetta 2005), it remains that this variable a priori seems not to be a crucial factor in ensuring private sector R&D, especially given its low correlation with the other candidate regressors. A possible explanation may also be that in many cases where the literature points to the need for flexible labor relations, this does not necessarily apply to wages but may refer, for example, to the ease with which researchers can participate as officers in start-ups related to their work.

Last, but not least, one has to stress the importance of the educational system for the third tier, as well as for the first tier, though with a relatively low positive coefficient (the negative coefficient in tier 2 is very small). In addition, one should note that in spite of the significant differences in the averages of the groups, as well as other differences, such as the behavior of the residuals, the estimated parameters for the variables present in the subgroups—for example, venture capital availability and the quality of research institutions—appear in many cases to be impressively similar in the final specifications treated for multicollinearity and heteroscedasticity. This outcome seems compatible with the nonadoption of the seemingly unrelated regression model.

Overall, the quality of certain institutional and policy variables, including the quality of the educational system (which also is largely determined by public policies), is positively correlated with factors ranging from the intensity of domestic competition (and the highly correlated breadth of value chain) to the quality of (often publicly funded) research institutions that appear to play a pivotal role in whether the private sector invests money in R&D. In turn, the availability of venture capital also places high exigencies on the policy environment, something documented both from this analysis and the literature survey. Therefore, given the low level of business R&D expenditure in Greece and the existence of relatively competent research centers that constitute a key enabling factor, the importance of a broad spectrum of policies associated with the establishment of a business-friendly and stable environment should be acknowledged by Greek policymakers, especially when setting targets for increased business spending on R&D.

Policy Proposals

The situation of Greece with respect to the issues identified by the preceding analysis points to some concrete proposals that can be introduced relatively easily, possibly merely by the enactment of good laws that encourage formation of stronger linkages between the business community and the existing research establishment. It should be added here that the following policy proposals have been examined in debates and interviews with numerous representatives of the Greek research and business communities during the past five years.

Based on the data analysis, we make the following general proposals for Greece:

—Despite its existing research capacity and significant physical infrastructure, Greece scores poorly in innovation and competitiveness, especially with respect to government regulations and practices that curtail competition. The practices in particular should be addressed quickly to give businesses the incentive to make use of the country's existing research resources.

—The breadth of the value chain is important, which advises against single-dimensional growth strategies that focus only on one sector (for example, tourism) and supports encouragement of a greater range of economic activity, which must include manufacturing.

—Financing for innovative projects is a problem, one that needs to be fixed comprehensively. Therefore institutions to support such financing from the private sector need to be established, or existing ones need to be enhanced to address this problem, even while the recovery of the whole financial system is given top priority as a precondition for the success of these niche financial products.

—Respect for property and intellectual property needs to be a policy priority, not only to support the development of these financial services but also to encourage innovation in general.

—Overall governance needs to improve.

More detailed recommendations can be based on eliminating the deficiencies identified in box 3-2.

Other important and relevant reforms are linked to these proposals. One is reform of tertiary education by increasing the autonomy and accountability of tertiary education institutions (see Mitsopoulos and Pelagidis 2010b) and ending their dependence on forces that significantly impede their academic performance. Unfortunately, this process is not only still incomplete but has partly retrogressed.

Another associated area in need of reform is the licensing and tax treatment of innovative activities, which is not explicitly permitted by the arcane Greek laws. Building on the important ongoing reforms, especially in the area of licensing, innovative enterprises need to be accommodated, within reasonable bounds, rather than discouraged by obstacles imposed by a sclerotic bureaucracy.

Conclusions

Because of numerous institutional hurdles, expensive and often very high quality state-sponsored research facilities are discouraged from transferring their knowledge to Greek companies. This wasted potential is simply intolerable, especially since these centers of expertise can play a crucial role in developing innovations that will stimulate and improve economic activity in sectors that have a history of success in Greece.

While Greece does have some strengths, including the aforementioned research capacity and a modern physical infrastructure, crucial shortcomings persist in areas ranging from the educational system to effective

Box 3-2. *Preconditions for Business Investment in R&D versus Current Status in Greece, 2014*

Preconditions	Status
Competitive upstream markets	Despite some progress, still not ensured as legislation still protects professional groups and mainly state-owned, or sponsored, incumbents.
Competitive downstream markets	Despite some progress, still not ensured as legislation still protects professional groups and mainly state-owned, or sponsored, incumbents.
Ability to freely form production process	Numerous regulations still do not permit it.
Ability to freely choose input mix	Numerous regulations still do not permit it.
Sanctity of contracts	Legal ambiguity, slow courts, and unpredictable legislation have undermined it and still do so.
Protection of property	Legal ambiguity, slow courts, and unpredictable legislation have undermined it and still do so. Unpredictable taxation also adds to this problem.
Contracting expertise (legal, accounting, and the like)	Generally at a low level; technology transfer centers often have only piecemeal access to the necessary expertise. The situation has been exacerbated by budget cuts that have curtailed the use of the limited resources available.
Expertise (scientific and legal) to write good patents	Legislation limits practice in this market to lawyers, who usually lack the scientific background to write strong patents in cases that are more technically challenging. A legal framework for training scientists in this capacity, especially if it would set standards similar to European and U.S. practices, could create significant opportunities.
Courts that can uphold intellectual property rights	The expertise is lacking in the courts. In addition, they are being restructured at this writing, and given their slow procedures, the results of the ongoing changes must be assessed. Specialized courts have recently been established and form an important starting point for addressing these inadequacies.
Flexibility to adapt to international standards	Presently it is low, especially since for many activities the Greek state does not accept the standards and the results of certified laboratories from other EU countries. Certification of professions, skills, and conformity with standards also poses a significant problem in many areas.
Support services for all parties to help them resolve issues that are not their field of expertise	Some infrastructure exists, but scarcity of funds endangers it.

Preconditions	Status
Ability to vest the intellectual property with limited liability and to freely transfer shares through an entity that is easy and inexpensive to set up and maintain	Many problems still exist despite legislation to reduce minimum capital requirements for some company types, a complicated law to create a new type of limited liability company, and the setup of one-stop shops that operate under unnecessarily complicated processes.
Flexibility to decide distribution of rewards to stakeholders, employees, and other collaborators	Hampered by overly stringent rules and a very hostile tax environment that is extremely unpredictable, both as legislation and case law. Furthermore, numerous dormant and irrational articles from old tax laws are being suddenly and unpredictably activated by the tax authorities, and thereby causing further legislative uncertainty.
Flexibility to establish collaborations with respect to employment	Some relaxation of employment protection laws since 2012 that could also be pertinent to innovative start-ups. Some increased flexibility for employees of research centers to collaborate with companies. Similar flexibility for universities was planned but not enacted into law. Sufficient flexibility of academic staff to collaborate with companies on projects but significant restrictions on their ability to receive more than token remuneration.
Ability to use losses from unsuccessful endeavors to offset tax on profits from successful ones	Very hostile tax environment.
Ease and low cost for winding down unsuccessful endeavors	Not the case.
Ease of licensing the transfer of knowledge from centers where it is developed to potential users	Almost impossible until recently, both because the law was ambiguous and because it was simply impossible for companies to approach universities. Some improvements on the legislative front since December 2011, and slowly some change in mentality is occurring.

Source: Authors' evaluations based on literature review and interviews with Greek researchers and innovative businesses, especially those conducting research.

protection of intellectual property. There has been some change in mentality, encouraged by the success of some innovative projects. However, since government funding for innovative activity has essentially collapsed, the survival of such projects will depend increasingly on the ability to sell the resultant expertise to the markets. A new law now permits state-financed universities to establish research centers as separate legal entities that are able to negotiate the transfer of knowledge to interested businesses. This has increased the legal flexibility in arranging collaborations between research centers and the business sector—but not yet to a sufficient degree. Numerous obstacles still remain as a result of legal uncertainties. As Rodrik, Hausmann, and Hwang (2006) point out, if a given activity does not manage to thrive, it will sooner or later die out. This warning applies to the knowledge infrastructure of Greek research universities and associated clusters and science parks. The documented decline in human capital in Greece, indicating a widespread brain drain, should be taken as a serious danger signal. And in line with the results of our analysis, when any such activity dies out, it not only represents a primary loss to the economy, but more important, it lessens the complexity of the remaining economic activity in the country—a complexity that is needed to generate knowledge-intensive, high value added goods and services.

Actions to address the obstacles, shortcomings, and needs enumerated in this chapter must become top policy priorities—and soon. While some of these issues (for instance, the quality of education and the establishment of overall sound institutions and good governance) inevitably require long-term strategies, a number of the other problems identified here can be dealt with relatively quickly if effective policies are formulated and implemented in a decisive way. What is needed—and what so far has been missing—from the relevant Greek policies is a clear decision to facilitate, rather than obstruct, collaboration between the government-funded research institutions and the business sector. This entails a determined effort to properly implement details affecting the manner of collaboration, the institution of patent agents, the provision of an inexpensive and flexible form of legal entity, and the revamping of tax laws. In addition, the development of healthy niche markets to support the private financing of innovative research will depend on the financial markets, which must be allowed to recover, a respect for property rights, and the commitment of the official sector to deal with numerous lingering legislative issues. All of this and more are preconditions for a fruitful collaboration between the research and business sectors that will stimulate the Greek economy and help lead Greece out of its current fiscal and entrepreneurial doldrums.

Appendix A

Cases of Corruption in the Greek Government, 2008–12

The following reports are translated from the Greek.

2008

January 27: "100 Million Euro 'Siemens' Bribes to Political Parties and OTE Executives," *Kathimerini* (http://news.kathimerini.gr/4dcgi/_w_articles_ell_100079_27/01/2008_257145).

June 20: Papadiohou K. P., "Tsoukatos 'Confession' for Siemens," *Kathimerini* (http://news.kathimerini.gr/4dcgi/_w_articles_politics_2_20/06/2008_274654).

2010

March 28: Telloglou T., "Bribes Also for the Submarines," *Kathimerini* (http://news.kathimerini.gr/4dcgi/_w_articles_politics_100033_28/03/2010_395832).

May 27: "T. Mandelis Admits Guilt for Siemens Bribes," *Capital.gr.* (www.capital.gr/News.asp?id=977808).

2011

February 8: Telloglou T., "Spiegel: Bribes with Names for the Submarines," *Kathimerini* (http://news.kathimerini.gr/4dcgi/_w_articles_ell_5_08/02/2011_431780).

2012

April 8: Telloglou T., "The Rich Background of Siemens,"
Kathimerini (http://news.kathimerini.gr/4dcgi/_w_articles_
politics_1_08/04/2012_478491).

August 24: Telloglou T., "Compromise Signed with Siemens,"
Kathimerini (http://news.kathimerini.gr/4dcgi/_w_articles_
politics_2_24/08/2012_493299).

2013

February 12: Telloglou T., "New Court Summations for the Black
Funds of Siemens," *Kathimerini* (http://portal.kathimerini.
gr/4dcgi/_w_articles_kathbreak_1_12/02/2013_482845).

Appendix B

Data and Statistical Analysis

Table 1. *Separation of Countries into Three Subgroups by Government Effectiveness Indicator, 2011*

Tier 1	Tier 2	Tier 3
Australia	Argentina	Algeria
Austria	Armenia	Azerbaijan
Barbados	Bahrain	Bangladesh
Belgium	Botswana	Benin
Canada	Brazil	Bolivia
Chile	Bulgaria	Bosnia and Herzegovina
Cyprus	China	Burkina Faso
Czech Republic	Colombia	Burundi
Denmark	Costa Rica	Cambodia
Estonia	Croatia	Cameroon
Finland	El Salvador	Chad
France	Georgia	Dominican Republic
Germany	Greece	Ecuador
Hong Kong	Guyana	Egypt
Hungary	India	Ethiopia
Iceland	Indonesia	Gambia
Ireland	Italy	Guatemala
Israel	Jamaica	Honduras
Japan	Jordan	Kenya
Korea, Rep.	Kazakhstan	Kyrgyz Republic
Latvia	Kuwait	Madagascar

(*continued*)

Table 1 (*continued*)

Tier 1	Tier 2	Tier 3
Lithuania	Lesotho	Mali
Luxembourg	Macedonia	Mauritania
Malaysia	Mexico	Mongolia
Malta	Montenegro	Mozambique
Mauritius	Morocco	Nepal
Netherlands	Namibia	Nicaragua
New Zealand	Oman	Nigeria
Norway	Panama	Pakistan
Portugal	Peru	Paraguay
Qatar	Philippines	Russia
Singapore	Poland	Saudi Arabia
Slovak Republic	Puerto Rico	Senegal
Slovenia	Romania	Tajikistan
Spain	Serbia	Tanzania
Sweden	SouthAfrica	Timor-Leste
Switzerland	SriLanka	Uganda
Taiwan	Thailand	Ukraine
United Arab Emirates	Trinidad and Tobago	Venezuela
United Kingdom	Turkey	Zambia
United States	Uruguay	Zimbabwe

Source: World Bank, "Worldwide Governance Indicators" (http://info.worldbank.org/governance/wgi/index. aspx#home).

Table 2a. *Regressor Correlations for Subgroup 1 (Tier 1)*[a]

Tier 1		1*	2*	3	4	5	6	7	8	9	10	11	12	13	14	15	16	17
1	Property rights, 1–7 (best)	1.00																
2	Intellectual property protection, 1–7 (best)	0.87	1.00															
3	Burden of government regulation, 1–7 (best)	0.44	0.38	1.00														
4	Quality of overall infrastructure, 1–7 (best)	0.52	0.64	0.41	1.00													
5	**Quality of the educational system, 1–7 (best)**	0.71	0.77	0.49	0.48	**1.00**												
6	Intensity of local competition, 1–7 (best)	0.29	0.36	-0.10	0.32	0.23	1.00											
7	Burden of customs procedures, 1–7 (best)	0.55	0.56	0.59	0.48	0.42	0.18	1.00										
8	**Flexibility of wage determination, 1–7 (best)**	-0.32	-0.33	0.25	-0.18	-0.19	-0.09	-0.09	**1.00**									
9	**Venture capital availability, 1–7 (best)**	0.58	0.57	0.44	0.26	0.45	0.38	0.47	0.00	**1.00**								
10	Domestic market size index, 1–7 (best)	0.16	0.32	-0.25	0.34	0.03	0.65	-0.02	0.00	0.22	1.00							
11	**Value chain breadth, 1–7 (best)**	0.50	0.59	0.11	0.61	0.37	0.48	0.28	-0.30	0.33	0.52	**1.00**						
12	**Quality of scientific research institutions, 1–7 (best)**	0.48	0.66	0.06	0.45	0.56	0.47	0.19	-0.15	0.39	0.60	0.58	**1.00**					
13	Control of corruption: Estimate	0.81	0.83	0.36	0.55	0.66*	0.19	0.61	-0.36	0.44	0.13	0.34	0.48	1.00				
14	Government effectiveness: Estimate	0.80	0.84	0.38	0.64	0.73*	0.26	0.61	-0.33	0.47	0.20	0.48	0.60*	0.89	1.00			
15	Regulatory quality: Estimate	0.63	0.59	0.10	0.28	0.40	0.31	0.52	-0.23	0.40	0.25	0.34	0.46	0.72	0.76	1.00		
16	Rule of law: Estimate	0.77	0.77	0.13	0.45	0.60*	0.23	0.47	-0.44	0.34	0.21	0.40	0.53*	0.90	0.87	0.83	1.00	
17	Voice and accountability: Estimate	0.32	0.26	-0.40	0.07	0.10	0.04	0.00	-0.52*	-0.06	0.09	0.19	0.25	0.43	0.43	0.57	0.66	1.00

Source: Authors' calculations.
*Significant (> 0.50) correlations with variables not included among regressors.
a. Bold for both values and respective variable titles indicates retained regressors.

Table 2b. *Regressor Correlations for Subgroup 2 (Tier 2)*[a]

Tier 2	1*	2*	3	4	5	6	7	8	9	10	11	12	13	14	15	16	17
1 Property rights, 1–7 (best)	1.00																
2 Intellectual property protection, 1–7 (best)	0.86	1.00															
3 **Burden of government regulation, 1–7 (best)**	0.15	0.17	1.00														
4 **Quality of overall infrastructure, 1–7 (best)**	0.60	0.64	0.33	1.00													
5 **Quality of the educational system, 1–7 (best)**	0.16	0.22	0.30	0.05	1.00												
6 Intensity of local competition, 1–7 (best)	0.49	0.43	0.00	0.31	0.27	1.00											
7 Burden of customs procedures, 1–7 (best)	0.54	0.67	0.45	0.61*	0.17	0.31	1.00										
8 **Flexibility of wage determination, 1–7 (best)**	–0.01	–0.10	0.31	0.04	0.16	0.17	0.18	1.00									
9 Venture capital availability, 1–7 (best)	0.56	0.55	0.30	0.20	0.31	0.49	0.42	0.25	1.00								
10 Domestic market size index, 1–7 (best)	–0.05	0.02	–0.32	–0.13	–0.06	0.43	0.00	–0.22	0.12	1.00							
11 **Value chain breadth, 1–7 (best)**	0.21	0.30	–0.11	0.02	0.32	0.53	0.24	–0.09	0.27	0.53	1.00						
12 Quality of scientific research institutions, 1–7 (best)	0.33	0.38	–0.22	–0.02	0.37	0.40	0.02	–0.16	0.37	0.44	0.41	1.00					
13 Control of corruption: Estimate	0.50	0.48	0.00	0.35	0.12	0.10	0.42	–0.25	0.12	–0.23	0.05	0.12	1.00				
14 Government effectiveness: Estimate	0.53	0.58	0.04	0.55*	0.17	0.26	0.48	–0.24	0.14	0.04	0.25	0.27	0.64	1.00			
15 **Regulatory quality: Estimate**	0.41	0.42	–0.05	0.34	–0.05	0.20	0.44	0.07	0.13	–0.01	0.27	0.04	0.50	0.68	1.00		
16 Rule of law: Estimate	0.65	0.67	0.03	0.45	0.29	0.24	0.53	–0.19	0.28	–0.10	0.24	0.28	0.81	0.74	0.58*	1.00	
17 Voice and accountability: Estimate	–0.01	0.02	–0.54*	–0.20	–0.09	–0.02	–0.18	–0.48	–0.21	–0.02	0.13	0.22	0.41	0.32	0.34	0.29	1.00

Source: Authors' calculations.

*Significant (> 0.50) correlations with variables not included among regressors.

a. Bold for both values and respective variable titles indicates retained regressors.

Table 2c. *Regressor Correlations for Subgroup 3 (Tier 3)*[a]

Tier 3		1*	2*	3	4	5	6	7	8	9	10	11	12	13	14	15	16	17
1	Property rights, 1–7 (best)	1.00																
2	Intellectual property protection, 1–7 (best)	0.80	1.00															
3	**Burden of government regulation, 1–7 (best)**	0.64	0.59	1.00														
4	**Quality of overall infrastructure, 1–7 (best)**	0.42	0.62	0.40	1.00													
5	**Quality of the educational system, 1–7 (best)**	0.23	0.47	0.19	0.42	1.00												
6	**Intensity of local competition, 1–7 (best)**	0.63	0.48	0.31	0.42	0.35	1.00											
7	Burden of customs procedures, 1–7 (best)	0.62	0.63	**0.71***	0.58	0.19	0.49	1.00										
8	**Flexibility of wage determination, 1–7 (best)**	0.37	0.09	0.34	0.07	-0.02	0.27	0.23	1.00									
9	**Venture capital availability, 1–7 (best)**	0.37	0.47	0.22	0.47	0.31	0.30	0.20	0.17	1.00								
10	**Domestic market size index, 1–7 (best)**	0.09	0.07	-0.27	0.32	0.13	0.30	-0.11	0.01	0.37	1.00							
11	**Value chain breadth, 1–7 (best)**	0.54	0.56	0.38	0.63	0.30	0.55	0.49	0.29	0.59	0.29	1.00						
12	**Quality of scientific research institutions, 1–7 (best)**	0.48	0.54	0.17	0.39	0.60	0.48	0.14	0.08	0.44	0.32	0.39	1.00					
13	Control of corruption: Estimate	0.50	0.34	**0.29**	0.13	-0.05	0.36	0.42	0.09	0.14	0.02	0.20	0.18	1.00				
14	Government effectiveness: Estimate	0.59	0.41	**0.23**	0.38	0.17	**0.52***	0.35	0.23	0.32	0.39	0.39	0.44	0.63	1.00			
15	Regulatory quality: Estimate	0.60	0.39	**0.41**	0.30	0.07	**0.57***	0.52	**0.54***	0.28	0.18	**0.50***	0.32	0.53	0.70	1.00		
16	Rule of law: Estimate	0.69	0.50	**0.41**	0.22	0.05	**0.50***	0.49	0.33	0.18	0.13	0.33	**0.40**	0.77	0.73	0.73	1.00	
17	Voice and accountability: Estimate	-0.10	-0.30	**-0.12**	-0.37	-0.24	0.10	-0.02	0.00	-0.24	-0.15	-0.10	-0.13	0.29	0.21	0.28	0.23	1.00

Source: Authors' calculations.

*Significant (> 0.50) correlations with variables not included among regressors.

a. Bold for both values and respective variable titles indicates retained regressors.

Table 3. *Mean Values and Standard Deviations of Key WEF and World Bank Variables, 2011*

	Tier 1		Tier 2		Tier 3		
	Mean	STD	Mean	STD	Mean	STD	Greece
Company spending on R&D, 1–7 (best)	4.28	0.95	3.08	0.46	2.77	0.42	2.37
Property rights, 1–7 (best)	5.63	0.64	4.46	0.72	3.58	0.73	4.46
Intellectual property protection, 1–7 (best)	5.07	0.81	3.56	0.77	2.86	0.60	3.83
Burden of government regulation, 1–7 (best)	3.59	0.74	3.09	0.64	3.18	0.56	2.35
Quality of overall infrastructure, 1–7 (best)	5.53	0.78	3.88	0.89	3.04	0.77	4.48
Quality of the educational system, 1–7 (best)	4.73	0.80	3.52	0.56	3.11	0.65	2.85
Intensity of local competition, 1–7 (best)	5.51	0.38	4.83	0.52	4.29	0.55	4.64
Burden of customs procedures, 1–7 (best)	5.02	0.57	3.84	0.62	3.41	0.66	3.98
Flexibility of wage determination, 1–7 (best)	4.89	1.04	4.93	0.78	4.98	0.65	3.11
Venture capital availability, 1–7 (best)	3.67	0.79	2.89	0.56	2.41	0.45	2.18
Domestic market size index, 1–7 (best)	4.07	1.17	3.68	1.25	2.99	1.00	4.36
Value chain breadth, 1–7 (best)	4.78	0.82	3.61	0.54	3.08	0.49	3.34
Quality of scientific research institutions, 1–7 (best)	4.96	0.77	3.68	0.57	3.18	0.61	3.29
Control of corruption: Estimate −2.5 to 2.5 (best, approx.)	1.33	0.71	−0.09	0.45	−0.78	0.31	−0.15
Government effectiveness: Estimate −2.5 to 2.5 (best, approx.)	1.39	0.45	0.13	0.29	−0.74	0.28	0.48
Regulatory quality: Estimate −2.5 to 2.5 (best, approx.)	1.30	0.41	0.24	0.40	−0.57	0.43	0.51
Rule of law: Estimate −2.5 to 2.5 (best, approx.)	1.33	0.46	−0.05	0.45	−0.82	0.40	0.57
Voice and accountability: Estimate −2.5 to 2.5 (best, approx.)	0.99	0.63	0.07	0.66	−0.58	0.52	0.82

Source: Authors' calculations.

Table 4. *Regressions Explaining Business R&D Expenditure*

Independent variable	BERD Tier 1 (1)	BERD Tier 2 (2)	BERD Tier 3 (3)
Constant	−2.239***	0.121	0.048
	(0.435)	(0.216)	(0.195)
Burden of government regulation		0.122***	−0.075**
		(0.037)	(0.043)
Quality of overall infrastructure	0.053	−0.062***	−0.019
	(0.043)	(0.024)	(0.036)
Quality of the educational system	0.074**	−0.058*	0.176***
	(0.040)	(0.041)	(0.034)
Intensity of local competition	0.010	0.189***	0.170***
	(0.075)	(0.048)	(0.048)
Burden of customs procedures	−0.050		
	(0.053)		
Flexibility of wage determination	0.040*	−0.081***	−0.050*
	(0.028)	(0.029)	(0.032)
Venture capital availability	0.174***	0.103***	0.320***
	(0.039)	(0.042)	(0.052)
Domestic market size index		0.008	0.039**
		(0.021)	(0.023)
Value chain breadth	0.606***	0.216***	0.205***
	(0.042)	(0.048)	(0.057)
Quality of scientific research institutions	0.464***	0.395***	0.137***
	(0.046)	(0.043)	(0.041)
Control of corruption		0.001	−0.032
		(0.057)	(0.058)
Regulatory quality		−0.258***	
		(0.052)	
Voice and accountability	0.037		0.000
	(0.046)		(0.037)
R-square	*0.880*	*0.734*	*0.663*
Observations	*205*	*205*	*205*

Source: Authors' calculations based on data described in the text.

Notes: Robust standard errors (corrected for heteroscedasticity) in parentheses. Asterisks indicate statistical significance at the ***0.01, **0.05, or * 0.1 level.

Figure 1. *Correlation of WEF Perception Index for BERD and Eurostat BERD as a Percent of GDP, 2006–13*[a]

BERD as percent of GDP

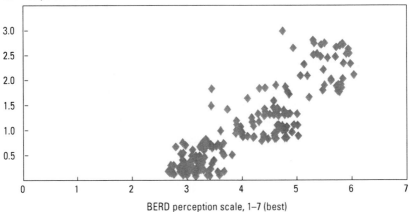

BERD perception scale, 1–7 (best)

Source: World Economic Forum (WEF) (www.weforum.org/issues/global-competitiveness); Eurostat (http://epp.eurostat.ec.europa.eu/portal/page/portal/statistics/search_database).

a. Countries with data available from both sources. BERD = business expendiure on R&D. Correlation coefficient: 0.885.

Figure 2. *Correlation of WEF Perception Index for BERD and WEF Perception Index for Industry-University Collaboration, 2006–13*[a]

Collaboration index, 1–7 (best)

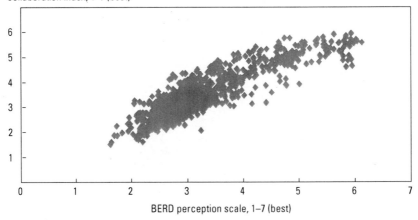

BERD perception scale, 1–7 (best)

Source: World Economic Forum (WEF) (www.weforum.org/issues/global-competitiveness).

a. BERD = business expendiure on R&D. Correlation coefficient: 0.8802.

Figure 3. *Correlation of WEF Perception Index for BERD and WEF Perception Index for Cluster Development, 2006–12*[a]

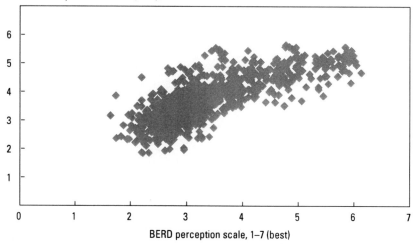

Cluster development index 1–7 (best)

BERD perception scale, 1–7 (best)

Source: World Economic Forum (WEF) (www.weforum.org/issues/global-competitiveness).
a. BERD = business expendiure on R&D. Correlation coefficient: 0.7801.

Notes

Introduction

1. Several recent studies, including one by McKinsey (2012a), already provide ample suggestions both for horizontal policies and for sector-specific policies. Furthermore, the numerous issues that need to be included in a comprehensive growth strategy for Greece are treated, among others, in studies by McKinsey (2012a, 2013) and the Boston Consulting Group (2013). They stress the contribution of the tourism and shipping sectors to the Greek economy, sectors often considered to be key parts of a strategy to achieve the recovery of the country.

Chapter 1

1. From the confidential information, only those pieces that can also be supported by publicly available information have been included in this text. The source for the enacted laws is the *Official Government Gazette, Issue A*, 1990, no.: 101, 124, 127, 138, 142, 143, 147, 157, 163, 178, 186; 1991, no.: 12, 19, 41, 50, 96, 114, 123, 132, 138, 146, 149, 167, 184, 192, 206; 1992, no.: 34, 42, 94, 104, 113, 123, 129, 130, 138, 154, 158, 159, 165, 180, 181; and 1993, no.: 15, 24, 48, 57, 62, 88, 109, 118, 127. All are available at www.et.gr.

2. How did public opinion in Greece view the European future of the country and the necessary reforms that would ensure its success? Polls and the *Eurobarometer* (EC 1992), even ahead of the ratification of the Maastricht Treaty, reveal for Greece a very high trust in the European institutions and a very low trust in the domestic political establishment when compared to the beliefs of the citizens of other European countries. One also has to keep in mind that in 1990 the government was elected on the basis of rhetoric that explicitly stated that structural reforms and fiscal consolidation were inevitable; that in 1996 the electorate voted

in a socialist government that appeared to have a credible chance of addressing the country's shortcomings, without the risks of a head-on confrontation with powerful special interest groups; and that in 2004 the electorate supported a government that had announced its intention to reform public administration and consolidate public finances. Thus all the available evidence appears to support the assertion that the electorate for decades had supported those candidates who, at each election, appeared more likely to secure the European future of the country and to address its perceived shortcomings, while at the same time looking to the European institutions as guarantors that would ultimately force the Greek political establishment to break with its previous habits of the past. See Mavris (2004) for a more detailed analysis.

3. Minutes from the 1992 discussion in the Greek parliament preceding the ratification of the Maastricht Treaty are available from the Hellenic Parliament Archives.

4. During this time the central government data in the budget were more reliable than those from general government entities, and therefore the budget did not always reflect the full extent of general government indebtedness. Also, after 1993 the GDP of the country was recalculated according to ESA95 (the European system of national and regional accounts) and found to be higher. Thus the data currently presented in the EC tables differs from the data included in the government's budgets at the time, as the deficits of the general government entities are added to the numbers and as the numerator of the deficit-to-GDP ratio has increased. See the annual budgets of the government for 1990 through1995, available in the library of the Bank of Greece and the Greek parliament. The increase in GDP implies that the deficit and debt ratios to GDP are now calculated to be smaller than shown in the tables of the government budgets for the years 1990–94.

5. According to the government's budget for the year 1994—submitted in November 1993 by the successor government, which had no motive to present facts that would favor its predecessor—the loans of "economic rationalization" provided during the previous decade and paid off during the 1991–92 period had added 1.897 billion drachmas to the public debt, or 11.2 percent of 1993 GDP ("Introduction to the 1994 Budget as Submitted to the Parliament," p. 127). In addition, the accumulated losses of the Bank of Greece (mainly from interventions to stabilize the drachma during the previous decade) came to 2.973 billion drachmas (17.7 percent of GDP), and these also were added to the public debt, as prescribed by the Maastricht Treaty ("Introduction to the 1994 Budget," p. 129). These facts are repeated in the 1995 budget and in the Bank of Greece annual report. The combined government loan debt and the debt of the central bank increased the public debt (mainly central government debt by contemporary standards) by 29 percent of GDP. The older annual reports of the Bank of Greece, as well as the government's budgets, are available in the library of the Bank of Greece.

6. The 1988 reform of the Structural Funds, in the context of a package of measures including the reform of the common agricultural policy and the

equilibrium of the Community budget, known as "Delors Package," aimed to improve integration of the various actions conducted under the banner of structural policies and to increase economic and social cohesion within the then Community.

7. For a specific definition of the concept of rent-seeking, see Hillman (2009). As for the application of the concept in Greece, see Mitsopoulos and Pelagidis (2009).

8. Country efficiency (overall productive performance) in terms of technical efficiency is measured by data envelopment analysis (DEA), a linear programming technique. Other work that uses DEA to rank the productive performance of entire nations includes Land, Lovell, and Thore (1994), Lovell (1993), and Chortareas, Pelagidis and Desli (2003).

9. See, respectively, www.worldbank.org/governance/wgi, www.doing business.org, www.oecd.org/economy/pmr, www.weforum.org/issues/global-competitiveness, www.transparency.org/research/cpi/overview.

10. OECD, "Product Market Regulation Database" (www.oecd.org/economy/pmr).

11. The relevant series is "Nominal compensation per employee: total economy (HWCDW)." See "AMECO—The Annual Macro-Economic Database of the European Commission's Directorate General for Economic and Financial Affairs" (http://ec.europa.eu/economy_finance/db_indicators/ameco/index_en.htm).

12. All available IMF Article IV missions to Greece, the chairman's summing up, and detailed staff reports for the period from 1990 to 2009 are available at the library of the Bank of Greece for earlier years and at www.imf.org for more recent years.

13. See note 12.

14. See the following speeches by the prime minister from 1990 to 1993: April 24, 1990, "Inaugural Policy Declarations of the New Government"; June 22, 1990, to parliament, discussion of 1990 budget; July 16, 1990, to parliament; December 21, 1990, to parliament, discussion of 1991 budget; December 20, 1991, to parliament, discussion of 1992 budget; January 29, 1992, to parliament; December 17, 1992, to parliament; May 20, 1993, to Hellenic Federation of Enterprises (SEV).

15. The 1994 staff report explicitly mentions, more than once, the potential for markets to react anxiously to the government's debt, and that this fear would manifest itself in Greece's balance of payments. The report then warns that "at some point, markets would doubt the government's ability to mobilize the resources necessary to service the debt, and financing would dry up" (IMF 1994, p. 7).

16. See the president's introductory statements to the press conferences following the Governing Council's monetary policy decisions, available online at the European Central Bank, "Press Conferences" (www.ecb.europa.eu/press/press conf/1998/html/index.en.html).

17. See note 16.

18. Public references to the letter include Featherstone, Kazamias, and Papadimitriou (2000).

Chapter 2

1. A bail-in occurs when a financial institution's creditors and depositors have to write off a portion of what the institution owes them, as a way to reduce that entity's debt burden.

2. The automotive sector exemplifies such institutional impediments. Private development of motor vehicles is almost impossible because the process of certifying prototypes in Greece, and thus legally operating and testing them or even selling them as produced items, is prohibitively complex, expensive, and legally uncertain. And, of course, the licensing of the manufacturing facilities also faced nearly insurmountable hurdles.

3. Eurostat, "Average Annual Gross Earnings by Economic Activity," NACE Rev. 2 (http://appsso.eurostat.ec.europa.eu/nui/show.do?dataset=earn_gr_nace2& lang=en).

4. See IKA, "Monthly Bulletin on Employment Statistics" (http://tinyurl.com/phabwr2).

5. It is not clear from the Eurostat tables whether unemployment benefits received by many seasonal employees in the sector during the winter season, when they are laid off, are included in these data.

6. The Eurostat data on energy prices, which include excise taxes, have also led to inaccurate conclusions in many cases. The reason is that large industrial energy consumers in most European countries have individual agreements with energy suppliers, and these agreements include, among other things, steep reductions in tariffs and special agreements on how to manage operations during times with high energy demand in the system. The price provisions of these agreements, together with the remaining arrangements, are considered industrial secrets and thus are not disclosed and not included in the data published by Eurostat, even though in many countries such agreements cover over 50 percent of industrial energy consumption. In Greece, on the other hand, all consumption of energy, at least until early 2014, was priced at the officially set prices published by Eurostat.

7. See data from the European Commission, "Taxation Trends in the EU" (http://ec.europa.eu/taxation_customs/taxation/gen_info/economic_analysis/tax_structures/index_en.htm).

8. For salaried employees social security contributions are a given percentage regardless of the salary up to a given level, which varies according to the date the employee was first enrolled (before or after 1993) and after that level they do not increase any more. In 1993 this level increased significantly, thus implying that contributions kept rising for much higher salaries.

9. According to a press release by the Ministry of Economy on December 11, 2013, the property taxes due and not paid on time increased from 500 million euros in December 2012 to 932 million euros in October 2013, the largest percentage increase in arrears among all taxes. See Ministry of Finance, "Press Releases" (www.minifn.gr); for data see http://tinyurl.com/p2h6tfu.

10. Regarding the disproportionate role of property as collateral in Greece, see the interview with Jeff Anderson, senior director for European affairs, Institute of International Finance, *Kathimerini* (Athens), November 28, 2013.

11. The terms of the EFSF loan include a ten-year derogation of interest payments that are added to the owed capital, and repayment of both the capital and the accumulated interest is to start after 2022. According to the ESA, though, these deferred interest payments are still added to the interest expenditure of each year. See EFSF, "FAQs" (www.efsf.europa.eu/attachments/faq_en.pdf).

12. Effectively the assistance offered to Greece has the form of a facility that will not burden the budgets of other member states. Thus also the ten- year derogation of interest payments on the EFSF loan is added to the stock of the loan that Greece will have to pay back.

13. A liquidity crisis may also mean "a shortage of money stocks for peripheral countries." We may assume that the member state A experiences a positive demand shock while another member state B experiences a negative one. Such shocks may reflect shifts in the preferences of consumers from outside the euro area and therefore changes in the demand for and prices of the given countries' products in international goods markets. This is very much the original argument of Mundell (1961). Country B's trade balance will deteriorate and present a deficit while country A's will present a surplus. Let it be assumed that country B is Greece and country A is Germany. In this case Greece's currency stock will decline as it finances its deficit in the trade balance. As a result, money stock in Germany increases and its interest rate declines while money stock in Greece decreases and its interest rate increases. The symmetric adjustment that occurs is unfavorable for Greece because it is forced to reduce money supply and accept a permanent recession. The symmetric system could deteriorate into an asymmetric one, as Germany may absorb the extra inflows by selling government bonds in the money market to avoid an unexpected surge of inflation. It is worth mentioning that Greece needs extra growth rates in order to reach the average EMU living standards. Assuming that peripheral countries are more vulnerable to shocks due to low productivity levels, a predominance of traditional sectors, less skilled human capital, and so on, and taking into account that, then, European Community money will dry up in the near future, the single currency may bring economic insecurity for the weak and vulnerable member states such as Portugal or Greece. Asymmetry is further enhanced by the variation in monetary transmission mechanisms across the euro area. Countries with a higher reliance on short-term bank credit (the southern EMU group) would be affected more intensely and

rapidly by interest rate changes in comparison to economies (such as Germany, Belgium, Austria, and the Netherlands) that rely more heavily on longer-term finance (Ramaswamy and Sloek 1997; Arestis, Chortareas, and Pelagidis 2007). While there is no formal definition of a depression, a decline in GDP over 20 percent during five years and an increase in unemployment of the magnitude observed in Greece seem to merit the use of this term rather than the term recession. This is true in particular if the developments regarding private sector access to finance are taken into account. It appears that at least to some extent in Greece a downward spiral that feeds on itself has entangled the financial sector and the private, nonfinancial economy.

14. Studies have shown that agents may be willing to punish those perceived to obtain unjustified gains even if it comes at a personal cost. See Zizzo and Oswald (2001).

15. "If angels were to govern men, neither external nor internal controls on government would be necessary" (Madison 1788).

16. The decline in financing of the general government in 2012 occurred when Greek banks incurred the losses of PSI2 but their supervisory capital was not able to be replenished by the Hellenic Financial Stability Fund (HFSF) because the process became entangled in the repeated Greek elections.

17. One alternative considered to address the shortage of financing for Greece's private economy, especially the small and medium enterprises, was something akin to the schemes for financing SMEs in France and Germany. See the ECB's quarterly report on the financing conditions of SMEs (http://tinyurl.com/ppvre2w). See also EC (2012a).

18. Relevant to the unique policy challenges such an environment poses, see IMF, "Economic Forum: Policy Response to Crises," panel discussion with Ben Bernanke, Stanley Fischer, Kenneth Rogoff, Lawrence H. Summers, and Olivier Blanchard, Fourteenth Jacques Polak Annual Research Conference, November 8, 2013 (www.imf.org/external/mmedia/view.aspx?vid=2821294542001). Taking into account that the exact circumstances differ, and without implying in any way that a collectivization of debts is necessary, we suggest that Alexander Hamilton (1790) also provides a good example of innovative thinking on how to deal with a depressed economy.

19. See last sentence in note above.

20. These insights were largely formulated during the event "Financing Companies. Solutions and Prospects" organized by SEV Hellenic Federation of Enterprises on January 15, 2014. See http://tinyurl.com/nkfundx.

Chapter 3

1. In this vein, see Hausmann and Hidalgo (2010), Hausmann and others (2011), and particularly Hausmann (2012).

2. These interviews occurred on numerous occasions linked with the organization of a research and innovation prize by Hellenic Federation of Enterprises (SEV) and Eurobank.

3. See "Mittel-management: Germany's Midsized Companies Have a Lot to Teach the World." *The Economist,* November 25, 2010 (www.economist.com/node/17572160).

4. See World Bank, "Doing Business" (www.doingbusiness.org).

5. *Patent and Trademark Laws Amendments of 1980,* P.L. 96-517.

6. See "Decline and Small. Small Firms Are a Big Problem for Europe's Periphery." *The Economist,* March 3, 2012 (www.economist.com/node/21548923).

7. World Bank, "What Are the 6 Dimensions of Governance Measured by the Worldwide Governance Indicators?" (http://info.worldbank.org/governance/wgi/index.aspx?fileName=table1.pdf#faq).

References

Afonso, A., and M. Aubyn. 2005. "Non-Parametric Approaches to Education and Health Efficiency in OECD Countries." *Journal of Applied Economics* 8, no. 2: 227–46.

Afonso A., L. Schuknecht, and V. Tanzi. 2005. "Public Sector Efficiency: An International Comparison." *Public Choice* 123, no. 3-4: 321–47.

Aghion, P., E. Bartelsman, E. Perotti, and S. Scarpetta. 2008. "Barriers to Exit, Experimentation and Comparative Advantage." RICAFE 2 Working Paper. London School of Economics and Political Science.

Akcigit, U., D. Hanley, and N. Serrano-Velarde. 2011. "Back to Basics: Private and Public Investment in Basic R&D and Macroeconomic Growth." *2011 Meeting Papers from Society for Economic Dynamics*, Paper 1196.

Akcigit, U., and W. Kerr. 2012. "Growth through Heterogeneous Innovations." U.S. Census Bureau Center for Economic Studies Paper CES-WP-12-08.

Arestis, P., G. Chortareas, and E. Desli. 2006. "Financial Development and Productive Efficiency in OECD Countries: An Explanatory Analysis." *The Manchester School* 74, no. 4: 417–40.

Arestis, P., G. Chortareas, and T. Pelagidis. 2007. "Asymmetries as Sources of Conflict in a Monetary Union." In *Advances in Monetary Policy and Macroeconomics*, edited by P. Arestis and G. Zezza, pp. 106–22. London: Palgrave MacMillan.

Arnold, J., and C. Schwellnus. 2008. "Do Corporate Taxes Reduce Productivity and Investment at the Firm Level? Cross-Country. Evidence from the Amadeus Dataset." OECD Economics Department Working Paper 641. OECD: Paris.

Arnold, J., G. Nicoletti, and S. Scarpetta. 2008. "Regulation, Allocative Efficiency and Productivity in OECD Countries: Industry and Firm-Level Evidence." OECD Economics Department Working Paper 616, Paris: OECD.

Arora, A., M. Ceccagnoli, and W. Cohen. 2007. "Trading Knowledge: An Exploration of Patent Protection and Other Determinants of Market Transactions in Technology and R&D." In *Financing Innovation in the United States, 1870 to Present*, edited by N. Lamoreaux and K. Sokoloff, pp. 365–403. MIT Press.

Attiki Odos. 2010. "Study among 9,200 Drivers: With Attiki Odos We Save Time." *Attiki Odos News Bulletin* 26.

Audretsch, D., M. Hülsbeck, and E. Lehmann. 2012. "Regional Competitiveness, University Spillovers, and Entrepreneurial Activity." *Small Business Economics* 39, no. 3: 587–601.

Bain and Company and Institute of International Finance. 2013. *Restoring Financing and Growth to Europe's SMEs. Four Sets of Impediments and How to Overcome Them*. Boston and Washington.

Balasubramanian, N., and J. Sivadasan. 2011. "What Happens When Firms Patent? New Evidence from U.S. Economic Census Data." *Review of Economics and Statistics* 93, no. 1: 126–46.

Baldwin, R. 2006. "In or Out? Does It Matter? An Evidence-Based Analysis of the Trade Effects of the Euro." London: Center for Economic Policy Research. June.

Bartelsman, E., J. Haltiwanger, and S. Scarpetta. 2009. "Cross-Country Differences in Productivity: The Role of Allocative Efficiency." NBER Working Paper 15490. Cambridge, Mass.: National Bureau for Economic Research.

Bassanini, A., and S. Scarpetta. 2001. "Does Human Capital Matter for Growth in OECD Countries? Evidence from Pooled Mean-Group Estimates." OECD Economics Department Working Paper 282. Paris: OECD.

Bassanini, A., S. Scarpetta, and I. Visco. 2000. "Knowledge, Technology and Economic Growth: Recent Evidence from OECD Countries." OECD Economics Department Working Paper 259. Paris: OECD.

Baumol, W., and R. Strom. 2010. "Useful Knowledge of Entrepreneurship: Some Implications of History." In *The Invention of Enterprise: Entrepreneurship from Ancient Mesopotamia to Modern Times*, edited by D. Landes, J. Mokyr, and W. Baumol, pp. 527–42. Princeton University Press.

Boston Consulting Group. 2013. *Impact Assessment of the Shipping Cluster on the Greek Economy and Society*. October.

Bravo Biosca, A. 2010. *Growth Dynamics. Exploring Business Growth and Contraction in Europe and the US*. NESTA research report. London: National Endowment for Science, Technology and the Arts. November.

Cai, J., and N. Li. 2012. "Growth through Inter-sectoral Knowledge Linkages." Paper presented at the Econometric Society Winter Meeting, Chicago, January 6–8.

Chortareas, G., T. Pelagidis, and E. Desli. 2003. "Trade Openness and Aggregate Productive Efficiency." *European Research Studies* 6, no. 1: 193–201.

Conway, P., and G. Nicoletti. 2006. "Product Market Regulation in the Non-manufacturing Sectors of OECD Countries: Measurement and Highlights." OECD Economics Department Working Paper 530. Paris: OECD.

Cornell University, INSEAD, and WIPO. 2013. *The Global Innovation Index 2013: The Local Dynamics of Innovation.* Geneva, Ithaca, N.Y., and Fontainebleau, France.

Da Rin, M., M. Di Giacomo, and A. Sembenelli. 2011. "Entrepreneurship, Firm Entry, and the Taxation of Corporate Income: Evidence from Europe." *Journal of Public Economics* 95, no. 9-10: 1048–66.

Darby, L., and M. Zucker. 2007. "Real Effects of Knowledge Capital on Going Public and Market Valuation." In *Financing Innovation in the United States, 1870 to the Present,* edited by N. Lamoreaux and K. Sokoloff, pp. 433–68. MIT Press.

De Kok, J., P. Vroonhof, W. Verhoeven, N. Timmermans, T. Kwaak, J. Snijders, and F. Westhof. 2011. *Do SMEs Create More and Better Jobs?* Zoetermeer, Netherlands: EIM Business and Policy Research.

Desli E., and E. Chatzigiannis. 2011. "EU27 State versus Regional Efficiency." Paper presented at European Economics and Finance Society Tenth International Meeting, London, June 9–12.

Desli E., and T. Pelagidis. 2012. "On the Greek Debt." *International Papers in Political Economy,* May.

Djankov, S., R. La Porta, F. Lopez-de-Silanes, and A. Shleifer. 2002. *The Practice of Justice.* World Bank Development Report. Washington: World Bank.

Duval, R., and J. Elmeskov. 2005. "The Effects of EMU on Structural Reforms in Labor and Product Markets." OECD Economics Department Working Paper 438. Paris: OECD.

EC (European Commission). 1992. *Eurobarometer: Public Opinion in the European Community,* no. 37-38, June-December. Brussels.

———. 2000. *Report from the Commission: Convergence Report 2000.* COM(2000) 277 final. Brussels.

———. 2002. *2002 Broad Economic Policy Guidelines.* Brussels.

———. 2003. *Commission Recommendation on the Broad Guidelines of the Economic Policies of the Member States and the Community (for the 2003–2005 Period).* Brussels.

———. 2004. *Commission Recommendation on the 2004 Update of the Broad Guidelines of the Economic Policies of the Member States and the Community (for the 2003–2005 Period).* Brussels.

———. 2006a. *Greece. Assessment of National Reform Program 2005–2008.* Brussels.

———. 2006b. "Measuring Administrative Costs and Reducing Administrative Burdens in the European Union." Commission Working Document COM(2006) 691 final, 14.11.2006. Brussels.

———. 2008. *Innovation Union Scoreboard 2008.* Brussels (http://ec.europa.eu/enterprise/policies/innovation/files/proinno/eis-2008_en.pdf.).

———. 2009. Recommendation for a Council Recommendation on the 2009 Update of the Broad Guidelines for the Economic Policies of the Member States and the Community and on the Implementation of Member States' Employment Policies. 28.1.2009 COM(2009) 34 final. Brussels.

———. 2011a. "EU Economic Governance 'Six-Pack' Enters into Force." Memo-11-898. December (http://tiny.cc/1ailew).

———. 2011b. *Innovation Union Scoreboard 2011*. Brussels (http://ec.europa.eu/enterprise/policies/innovation/files/ius-2011_en.pdf

———. 2012a. "Overview of Competitiveness in 27 Member States." Memo. October 10.

———. 2012b. "The Contribution of Taxes to Fiscal Consolidation in the Euro Area." *Quarterly Report on the Euro Area* 11, no. 1.

———. 2013a. Directorate General for Economic and Financial Affairs. *General Government Data: General Government Revenue, Expenditure, Balances and Gross Debt*. Autumn (http://ec.europa.eu/economy_finance/db_indicators/gen_gov_data/time_series/index_en.htm).

———. 2013b. *Innovation Union Scoreboard 2013*. Brussels (http://ec.europa.eu/enterprise/policies/innovation/files/ius-2013_en.pdf), p.10.

———. 2013c. "The Second Economic Adjustment Program for Greece. Third Review–July 2013." Occasional Paper 159. Brussels.

ECB (European Central Bank). 2012. "Quarterly Euro Area Bank Lending Survey." Frankfurt. July.

EMI (European Monetary Institute). 1996. *Progress towards Convergence Report*. Frankfurt. November.

———. 1998. *Convergence Report*. Frankfurt. March.

European Council. 2002, *Recommendations on the Broad Guidelines of the Economic Policies of the Member States and the Community*. Brussels. (http://eur-lex.europa.eu).

———. 2003. *Recommendation on the Broad Guidelines of the Economic Policies of the Member States and the Community.*

———. 2007. *Recommendation on the Broad Guidelines of the Economic Policies of the Member States and the Community.*

———. 2008. *Recommendation on the Broad Guidelines of the Economic Policies of the Member States and the Community.*

———. 2009. *Recommendation on the Broad Guidelines of the Economic Policies of the Member States and the Community.*

———. 2010. "Council Recommendation to Greece of 16 February 2010." *Official Journal of the European Union*, L83, March 30, pp. 65–69 (http://eur-lex.europa.eu/LexUriServ/LexUriServ.do?uri=OJ:L:2010:083:0065:0069:EN:PDF)

———. 2011a. "Euro Summit Statement 2011." Brussels. October 26 (www.consilium.europa.eu/uedocs/cms_data/docs/pressdata/en/ec/125644.pdf).

———. 2011b. "Statement by the Heads of State or Government of the Euro Area and EU Institutions." Brussels. July 21 (www.consilium.europa.eu/uedocs/cms_data/docs/pressdata/en/ec/123978.pdf).

Fabrizio, K., and D. Mowery. 2007. "The Federal Role in Financing Major Innovations: Information Technology during the Postwar Period." In *Financing Innovation in the United States, 1870 to the Present*, edited by N. Lamoreaux and K. Sokoloff, pp. 283–316. MIT Press.

Featherstone, K., G. Kazamias, and D. Papadimitriou. 2000. "Greece and the Negotiation of Economic and Monetary Union: Preferences, Strategies, and Institutions." *Journal of Modern Greek Studies* 18: 393–414.

Gibson, H., and J. Malley. 2007. "The Contribution of Sectoral Productivity Differentials to Inflation in Greece." Working Paper 63. Athens: Bank of Greece.

Graham, M. 2007. "Financing Fiber." In *Financing Innovation in the United States, 1870 to the Present*, edited by N. Lamoreaux and K. Sokoloff, pp. 247–82. MIT Press.

———. 2010. "Entrepreneurship in the United States, 1920–2000." In *The Invention of Enterprise: Entrepreneurship from Ancient Mesopotamia to Modern Times*, edited by D. Landes, J. Mokyr, and W. Baumol, pp. 401–42. Princeton University Press.

Greene, W. 2007. *Econometric Analysis*. Upper Saddle River, N.J.: Prentice Hall.

Griffith, R., H. Harrison, and H. Simpson. 2006. "The Link between Product Market Reform, Innovation and EU Macroeconomic Performance." Washington: Institute for Fiscal Studies.

Gulbranson, C., and D. Audretsch. 2008. "Proof of Concept Centers: Accelerating the Commercialization of University Innovation." Kansas City, Mo.: Ewing Marion Kauffman Foundation. January.

Hajkova, D., G. Nicoletti, L. Vartia, and K.-Y. Yoo. 2007. "Taxation, Business Environment and FDI Location in OECD Countries." *OECD Economic Studies* 43 (1).

Haltiwanger, J., R. Jarmin, and J. Miranda. 2009. "Business Dynamics Statistics Briefing: Jobs Created from Business Startups in the United States." January 1 (http://ssrn.com/abstract=1352538 or http://dx.doi.org/10.2139/ssrn.1352538).

Hamilton, A. 1790. *First Report on Public Credit*. U.S. Treasury Department. January 9.

Hausman, N. 2012. "University Innovation, Local Economic Growth, and Entrepreneurship." U.S. Census Bureau Center for Economic Studies Paper CES-WP- 12-10. June.

Hausmann, R. 2012. "Ireland Can Show Greece a Way out of the Crisis." *Financial Times*, February 8.

Hausmann, R., and C. Hidalgo. 2010. "Country Diversification, Product Ubiquity, and Economic Divergence." Scholarly Article 4554740. Harvard University, Kennedy School of Government.

Hausmann, R., C. Hidalgo, S. Bustos, M. Coscia, C. Chung, C., J. Jimenez, A. Simoes, and M. Yildirim. 2011. *The Atlas of Economic Complexity. Mapping Paths to Prosperity*. Cambridge, Mass.: Puritan Press.

Hellenic Federation of Enterprises. 2007. "The Credibility of Corruption and Quality of Governance Indices." *Competitiveness Bulletin*, no. 46.

Henderson, D. J., and V. Zelenyuk. 2007. "Testing for Efficiency Catching-up." *Southern Economic Journal* 73, no. 4: 1003–19.

Hillman, A. 2009. *Public Finance and Public Policy: Responsibilities and Limitations of Government.* Cambridge University Press.

IMF. 1994. *Staff Report for 1994 Article IV Consultation.* Washington. June 16.

Jaffe, A., and J. Lerner. 2001. "Reinventing Public R&D: Patent Policy and the Commercialization of National Laboratory Technologies." *RAND Journal of Economics* 32, no. 1: 167–98.

Judge, G., R. Hill, W. Griffiths, H. Lütkepohl, and T. Lee. 1982. *Introduction to the Theory and Practice of Econometrics.* New York: John Wiley and Sons.

Kaufmann, D., and A. Kraay. 2006. "Measuring Governance Using Cross-Country Perceptions Data." In *International Handbook on the Economics of Corruption*, edited by S. Rose-Ackerman, pp. 52–104. Cheltenham, U.K.: Edward Elgar.

Kaufmann, D., A. Kraay, and M. Mastruzzi. 2005. *Governance Matters IV: Governance Indicators for 1996–2004.* Washington: World Bank.

Kirkegaard, J.-F. 2014. "The European Central Bank Remains on Hold." Peterson Institute for International Economics. March 5 (http://blogs.piie.com/realtime/?p=4247).

Kitson, M., and J. Michie. Forthcoming. "The Deindustrial Revolution: The Rise and Fall of UK Manufacturing, 1870–2010." In *The Cambridge Economic History of Modern Britain*, vol. 2, edited by R. Floud and P. Johnson. Cambridge University Press (http://michaelkitson.files.wordpress.com/2013/03/kitson-and-michie-the-deindustrial-revolution-web.pdf).

Krugman, P. 1993. "Lessons of Massachusetts for EMU." In *Adjustment and Growth in the European Monetary Union*, edited by F. Torres and F. Giavazzi, pp. 241–59. Cambridge University Press.

Lambsdorff, J. Graf. 2006. "Causes and Consequences of Corruption: What Do We Know from a Cross-Section of Countries?" In *International Handbook on the Economics of Corruption*, edited by S. Rose-Ackerman, pp. 3–51. Cheltenham, U.K.: Edward Elgar.

Lamoreaux, N., and K. Sokoloff, eds. 2007. *Financing Innovation in the United States, 1870 to the Present.* MIT Press.

Land K. C., C. A. K. Lovell, and S. Thore. 1994. "Productive Efficiency under Capitalism and State Socialism: An Empirical Inquiry Using Chance-Constrained Data Envelopment Analysis." *Technological Forecasting and Social Change* 46 (2): 139–52.

Lerner, J. 2007. "The Governance of New Firms: A Functional Perspective." In *Financing Innovation in the United States, 1870 to Present*, edited by N. Lamoreaux and K. Sokoloff, pp. 405–32. MIT Press.

————. 2009. *Boulevard of Broken Dreams: Why Public Efforts to Boost Entre-preneurship and Venture Capital Have Failed—and What to Do About It.* Princeton University Press.

————. 2012. *The Architecture of Innovation: The Economics of Creative Orga-nizations.* Cambridge, Mass.: Harvard Business Review Press.

Locke, R., and R. Wellhausen, eds. 2014. *Production in the Innovation Economy.* MIT Press.

Lovell, C. A. K. 1993. "Production Frontiers and Production Efficiency." In *The Measurement of Productive Efficiency: Techniques and Applications,* edited by H. Fried, C. A. K. Lovell, and S. Schmidt, pp. 3–67. Oxford University Press.

Maddison, A. 1995. *Monitoring the World Economy, 1820–1992.* Paris: OECD.

Madison, J. 1788. "The Structure of the Government Must Furnish the Proper Checks and Balances between the Different Departments." *The Federalist,* no. 51 (February 6).

Malliaropoulos, D. 2011. "The Loss of Competitiveness after the Country's EMU Accession." [In Greek.] In *The International Crisis in the Euro Area and the Greek Financial System,* edited by G. Hardouvelis and C. Gkortsos, pp. 359–76. Athens: Hellenic Bank Association.

Mavris, Y. 2004. "From Accession to the Euro. Evolution of the Greek Public Attitudes toward European Integration, 1981–2001." In *Greece in the EU,* edited by D. Dimitrakopoulos and A. Passas, pp. 113–38. London: Routledge.

McKinsey and Company. 2012a. *Greece 10 Years Ahead. Defining Greece's New Growth Model and Strategy.* Athens.

————. 2012b. McKinsey Global Institute. *Manufacturing the Future: The Next Era of Global Growth and Innovation.* New York.

————. 2013. *Tourism Strategic Planning 2021.* Athens.

Ministry of Transport. 2006. "Results of Study on Public Transport." Athens: MARC AE Marketing Research Communication.

Mitsopoulos, M. 2014. "Manufacturing, Competition and Business Environment. Removal of Obstacles—Opening to International Competition." In *Competi-tiveness for Growth: Policy Proposals,* edited by C. Gortsos and M. Massoura-kis. Athens: Hellenic Bank Association.

Mitsopoulos M., and T. Pelagidis. 2007. "Does Staffing Affect the Time to Serve Justice in Greek Courts?" *International Review of Law and Economics* 27, no. 2: 219–44.

————. 2009. "Vikings in Greece: Kleptocratic Interest Groups in a Closed, Rent-Seeking Economy." *Cato Journal* 29, no. 3: 399–416.

————. 2010a. "Greek Appeals Courts' Quality Analysis and Performance." *European Journal of Law and Economics* 30, no. 1: 17–39.

————. 2010b. "The Case for Abolishing the Higher Education State Monopoly in Continental Western Europe." *Journal of Economic Studies* 37, no. 1: 36–52.

————. 2011. *Understanding the Crisis in Greece.* London: Palgrave MacMillan.

―――. 2012. *Understanding the Crisis in Greece.* Rev. ed. London: Palgrave MacMillan.

Moomaw, R., and L. Adkins. 2000. "Regional Technical Efficiency in Europe." Working paper. Oklahoma State University.

Mundell, R. 1961. "A Theory of Optimum Currency Areas." *American Economic Review* 51, no. 4: 657–65.

Mylonas, P., and G. Papaconstantinou. 2001. "Product Market Reforms in Greece: Policy Priorities and Prospects." In *Greece's Economic Performance and Prospects*, edited by R. Bryant, N. Garganas, and G. Tavlas, pp. 499–544. Brookings.

Nicodème, G., and J-.B. Sauner-Leroy. 2004. "Product Market Reforms and Productivity: a Review of the Theoretical and Empirical Literature on the Transmission Channels." European Economy Economic Paper 218. Brussels: European Commission, Directorate General Economic and Monetary Affairs.

Nicoletti, G., and S. Scarpetta. 2005. "Product Market Reforms and Employment in OECD Countries." OECD Economics Department Working Paper 472. Paris: OECD.

OECD. 2009. "Structural Reform at a Time of Financial Crisis." In *Economic Policy Reforms 2009: Going for Growth*, chap. 1. Paris.

―――. 2010. "Tax Policy Reform and Economic Growth." Tax Policy Study no. 20. Paris. November.

―――. 2011a. *Financing High-Growth Firms: The Role of Angel Investors.* Paris.

―――. 2011b. "Housing and the Economy." In *Economic Policy Reforms 2011: Going for Growth*, chap. 4. Paris.

―――. 2011c. *OECD Science, Technology and Industry Scoreboard 2011: Innovation and Growth in Knowledge Economies.* Paris.

―――. 2012a. *Entrepreneurship at a Glance 2012.* Paris.

―――. 2012b. "Taxes on Property" (http://tinyurl.com/o9a5dal).

―――. 2013a. *Entrepreneurship at a Glance 2013.* Paris.

―――. 2013b. *OECD Competition Assessment Reviews: Greece.* Paris.

Paterson, I., M. Fink, and A. Ogus. 2003. "Economic Impact of Regulation in the Field of Liberal Professions in Different Member States, Regulation of Professional Services." Final Report, Part 3. Vienna: Institute for Advanced Studies. January.

Pelagidis, T. 2008. "Human Resource Development within Greek Science and Technology Parks Spin-offs." *Human Resources Development International* 11, no. 2: 207–14.

Pelagidis, T., and T. Toay. 2007. "Expensive Living: The Greek Experience under the Euro." *InterEconomics. Review of European Economic Policy* 42, no. 3: 167–76.

Persson, T., and G. Tabellini. 1996. "Monetary Cohabitation in Europe." CEPR Working Paper 1380. London: Center for Economic Policy Research. May.

Ramaswamy, R., and T. Sloek. 1997. "The Real Effects of Monetary Policy in the European Union: What Are the Differences?" Working Paper 160. Washington: IMF. December.

Rodrik, D. 2007. *One Economics, Many Recipes: Globalization, Institutions and Economic Growth.* Princeton University Press.

————. 2012. *The Globalization Paradox: Democracy and the Future of the World Economy.* Reprint. New York: W.W. Norton.

Rodrik, D., R. Hausmann, and J. Hwang. 2006. "What You Export Matters." CEPR Discussion Paper 5444. London: Center for Economic Policy Research.

Rose-Ackerman, S., ed. 2006. *International Handbook on the Economics of Corruption.* Cheltenham, U.K.: Edward Elgar.

Smith, A. 1776. *An Inquiry into the Nature and Causes of the Wealth of Nations.*

Soros, G. 2012. "The Tragedy of the European Union and How to Resolve It." *New York Review of Books,* September 27.

Stangler, D., and R. Litan. 2009. "Firm Formation and Economic Growth. Where Will The Jobs Come From?" Kauffman Foundation Research Series. Kansas City, Mo.: Ewing Marion Kauffman Foundation.

Stobbe, A., and P. Pawlicki. 2012. "Greece, Ireland, Portugal. More Growth via Innovation." *EU Monitor.* Frankfurt: Deutsche Bank.

Sutherland, D., and R. Price. 2007. "Linkages between Performance and Institutions in the Primary and Secondary Education Sector." OECD Economics Department Working Paper 558. Paris: OECD.

Trichet, J.-C. 2012. "Lessons from the Crisis: Challenges for the Advanced Economies and for the European Monetary Union." Eleventh Annual Niarchos Lecture, Peterson Institute for International Economics, Washington, May 17.

Workers Center of Athens. 1997. "Study on Commuting Conditions of Workers within the Workers Center of Athens."

World Economic Forum. 2013. *Manufacturing for Growth Strategies for Driving Growth and Employment,* vols. 1–3. Geneva.

Wunsch-Vincent, S. 2012. "Accounting for Science-Industry Collaboration in Innovation: Existing Metrics and Related Challenges." In *The Global Innovation Index 2012: Stronger Innovation Linkages for Global Growth,* edited by S. Dutta, pp. 97–107. Fountainebleau, France, and Geneva: INSEAD and World Intellectual Property Organization.

Zizzo D., and A. Oswald. 2001. "Are People Willing to Pay to Reduce Others' Incomes?" *Annales d'Economie et de Statistique,* no. 63-64: 39–62.

Index

Note: Boxes, figures, and tables are indicated by "b," "f," and "t" following page numbers.

ABOUT THE AUTHORS

Theodore Pelagidis is a professor of economics at the University of Piraeus, Greece and a nonresident senior fellow in Global Economy and Development at Brookings. He has also been a NATO scholar at the Center for European Studies of Harvard University, a Fulbright scholar at Columbia University and an NBG professorial fellow at the London School of Economics.

Michael Mitsopoulos is an economist at the Hellenic Federation of Enterprises, Greece, and has taught at the Economic University of Athens and the University of Piraeus. He holds a Ph.D. in Economics from Boston University.

Pelagidis and Mitsopoulos are co-authors of *Understanding the Crisis in Greece: From Boom to Bust* (Palgrave Macmillan, 2011).

Lightning Source UK Ltd.
Milton Keynes UK
UKOW01f1628220216

268871UK00003B/172/P